Managing Group Risk Attitude

Managing Group Risk Attitude

RUTH MURRAY-WEBSTER and
DAVID HILLSON

Routledge
Taylor & Francis Group
LONDON AND NEW YORK

First published in paperback 2024

First published 2008 by Gower Publishing

Published 2016 by Routledge
4 Park Square, Milton Park, Abingdon, Oxon OX14 4RN

and by Routledge
605 Third Avenue, New York, NY 10158

Routledge is an imprint of the Taylor & Francis Group, an informa business

British Library Cataloguing in Publication Data
Murray-Webster, Ruth
  Managing group risk attitude
  1. Risk management 2. Decision making
  I. Title II. Hillson, David, 1955–
  658.1'55

Library of Congress Cataloging-in-Publication Data
Murray-Webster, Ruth.
  Managing group risk attitude / by Ruth Murray-Webster and David Hillson.
    p. cm.
  Includes bibliographical references and index.
  ISBN 978-0-566-08787-5
  1. Risk management. I. Hillson, David, 1955– II. Title.

HD61.M87 2008
658.15'5--dc22

2007051244

ISBN 13: 978-0-566-08787-5 (hbk)
ISBN 13: 978-1-03-283795-6 (pbk)
ISBN 13: 978-1-315-59357-9 (ebk)

DOI: 10.4324/9781315593579

Contents

List of Figures

List of Tables

Acknowledgements

Our first book on risk attitudes was based on our shared understanding and experiences in the field, which had been shaped and informed by many people, including family and friends, colleagues and clients. Still, what we wrote then largely reflected our own perspectives, with their inherent limitations and biases. When we came to this book on group risk attitude, we wanted to ground it in the actual experiences and perceptions of people making real risky and important decisions in groups. As a result, this book combines our own views with the results of a two-phase research programme, and our main thanks go to those people who participated in our research.

Our first research phase collected detailed data on real decisions from a small number of organizations, as input to a rich interpretative study of the factors and influences operative in the decision-making group. Of course we know the identity of each person who contributed to our research, but they and their organizations are not named in the interests of protecting confidentiality. Candid observations on decisions of strategic importance were shared, and for this we are very grateful. You know who you are; our sincere thanks to each one of you.

The second phase was conducted using an anonymous web-based survey, drawing on our wide professional networks. Consequently the identity of our 281 online respondents is hidden even from us, but if you were one of them, we say a big thank you.

Of course, without the continued support of Jonathan Norman and his team at Gower Publishing you would not see our work in print. We are indebted to them for the opportunity to publish this latest instalment of our thinking on risk attitudes. Jonathan in particular has remained patiently encouraging, and seems to be genuinely interested in the topic!

Finally we acknowledge our deep gratitude to our families, who have always been (and will always be) the inspiration behind our work. Understanding and managing risk attitude is a challenge for anyone, but the people we most want to help are our children: Joshua, Helen, Kate, Tess and Mark. Hopefully they will read with interest, benefit from our endeavours, put it into practice, and change the world.

And to Fred and Liz, and our wider family and friends – another one finished, with your love and patience always with us. Thank you.

Ruth Murray-Webster and David Hillson

Foreword

The disciplines of risk management and stakeholder management are converging! The work of Ruth Murray-Webster and David Hillson has moved risk management away from an actuarial view towards the recognition that people's attitudes and emotions play a significant but manageable role in distinguishing between 'acceptable risks' and 'unacceptable risks'.

The synergy between the management of risk and the need to manage the relationships between organizations and their stakeholders is becoming increasingly evident in the work I do around the globe. The connections are threefold: firstly, most organizational risk is about people not cooperating, not delivering or not supporting the work being planned or undertaken. Secondly, it is people who make decisions about whether a risk is acceptable, how it should be managed or exploited, and who should manage it; these people are all subject to individual pressures and biases in making 'good' decisions and driving beneficial outcomes for their organization. Thirdly, the way an organization perceives risk, and the extent to which it is managed or ignored, is shaped and supported by the individuals and groups within the organization.

Historically, risk management has been seen as a rational, logical process and the application of risk management practices thought of as formulaic and procedural: only recently has the human element of risk started to receive proper recognition within many organizations. However, it is people who work the risk management process, it is people who are most often the source of risk, and it is people who decide what level of risk is 'acceptable'. Even the best way to manage risk is uncertain – it depends on how each risk is perceived, both by the people administering the risk management practices and by those who run the organization. The human element is central to the problem, and it is also central to the solution.

Thanks to the work of Murray-Webster and Hillson in this book and its predecessor *Understanding and Managing Risk Attitude,* the important connection between managing stakeholder relationships (people) and managing risk has been defined and clarified. Their first book analyzed the risk attitudes of individuals and groups; this book takes the next step by identifying the essential factors needed to make 'good decisions' in situations which are perceived as risky and important. Their research has identified three key elements of 'good' decision-making in groups, the first being the risk attitude of individuals, particularly those stakeholders who are powerful and who are close to the impact of the decision. The second key element includes the contextual and organizational norms that may bias the decision-making group, either consciously or unconsciously, while the third element describes group dynamics and shows how they may help or hinder an effective decision-making process.

An important factor in successfully managing group risk attitude is appreciating the impact of perception. Perception has long been understood as comprising a complex mix of the rational or 'conscious factors', 'subconscious factors' such as stereotyping and group-think, and 'affective factors' such as emotions or feelings. Here, the authors have developed an elegant representation of this complexity in the form of a *triple strand of influence*. Each of the three sets of influences, which together form the triple strand, is important in the context of decision-making; but they do not exist or operate in isolation. The strands interweave and combine to influence perception; and perception drives risk attitude, which in turn affects the quality of decisions made under conditions of uncertainty.

Appreciating 'perception' is only part of the journey. Murray-Webster and Hillson's new practitioner-based research also provides insights into how groups do, can and should manage risk. The authors had previously described 'the Four A's' of emotional literacy – a framework of Awareness, Appreciation, Assessment and Assertion. In this book another two 'A's' are added – Action and Acceptance, to create their new 'Six A's' model. This enhanced model is accompanied by practical guidance on how organizations can actively manage risk attitudes in uncertain group decision-making situations. The guidance parallels the core steps of standard risk processes, allowing these new insights to be easily absorbed into existing risk management practice.

The adaptation of approaches used in stakeholder analysis to group decision-making is another important contribution from the authors. Measuring the perceived levels of power or influence of individuals within the group, and assessing the degree of personal propinquity perceived by each individual (or 'how much it matters to them personally'), offers a model for understanding which individuals might exert the most influence on group risk attitude. These measures are an essential addition to other factors including: group dynamics; organizational culture; national culture; and societal norms that influence group behaviour and therefore shape the group's risk attitude.

A number of the key features of this book will enhance my own work in stakeholder relationship management, and contribute to my thinking about organizations, risk and stakeholders. These include the elegant 'triple strand' of influences, the 'Six A's' model of emotional literacy, and the adaptation of stakeholder analysis measures to understanding groups and how individuals operate in the group decision-making context. These ideas have already enriched my thinking, and I expect they will help other readers to appreciate the multi-faceted nature of risk and the importance of people in delivering successful outcomes.

The authors' practitioner-based research has led to the creation of practical guidelines for those seeking to improve risk management and group decision-making in their organization. There are many practical ideas to support the move away from a reactive approach to risk, towards one that acknowledges that there are many approaches to risk management and that the human element must be factored into every risk management decision. Anyone seeking information on how to make their risk management practices more effective, or how to encourage 'good' decision-making within groups, will find this book a goldmine.

Dr. Lynda Bourne DPM, PMP, MACS

Managing Director, Stakeholder Management Pty Ltd, Melbourne, Australia

Preface

If the doors of perception were cleansed, everything would appear to man as it is: infinite.

William Blake (1757–1827)

Since we started working together several years ago, we have discovered a shared fascination with two topics: risk and people. Of course these are not separate, since risk is identified, assessed and managed by people, not by processes or tools, but the relationship is more complex than that. People are both a source of risk exposure and part of the solution, and nearly every step in the risk process is influenced by perception: managing risk requires judgement.

Our previous work together has explored one key interface between the worlds of risk and people, namely risk attitudes. By taking the insights available from the field of emotional literacy, we have provided practical advice to enable anyone to understand and manage risk attitude, for themselves or for groups to which they belong. This book takes our work much further.

Most of what people do is accomplished through groups of one sort or another, and involves decision-making at various levels. Our continuing interest in risk and people has led us to examine this more closely, focusing on how people make decisions in groups, particularly when those decisions involve risk. Group risk attitude is a significant influence on both the decision process and the outcome, and if it is left unmanaged the consequences can be unpredictable. We have therefore conducted some research to explore how groups make risky decisions, focusing on the factors which influence risk attitudes, and our results have led to unexpected conclusions. The popular understanding of emotional literacy appears to be missing some crucial elements. Drawing on our deep experience of managing risk, we propose an extended framework to include explicit steps which allow group risk attitude in the decision-making context to be managed proactively.

We remain excited about the challenges of working in groups to understand and manage risk. We offer our findings to others who share our dual passion for risk and people, and we hope that our contribution makes a difference for those who are prepared to put it into practice.

Ruth Murray-Webster and David Hillson

PART I

Understanding and Managing Risk Attitude: The State of Current Knowledge

Understanding Risk Attitude

Dealing with risk for life and business

Life is full of risks. Every day people make decisions where the outcome matters but where the conditions surrounding the decision are more or less uncertain. Faced with these circumstances, most people have developed habits and strategies that enable their lives to 'free-flow' for much of the time. It is only in the presence of an unusual risk that people may be conscious of the need to make a choice.

The management of these uncertain situations that matter, also known as risk management, is a discipline in its own right. It has an established role in business, and is applied at a wide range of levels, including management of strategic risk, corporate governance, operational risk, project risk and health, safety and the environment (HSE). However, risk management is not just important for business. There is increasing interest in the application of effective risk management in society at large. A number of groups across government and academia have recognized the need for a more considered and responsible approach to risk, and highlight the urgent need for people to embrace 'appropriate risk-taking', both individually and in their working and social groups, supported by government and wider society.

By defining risk simply as 'uncertainty that matters', it is clear that knowing how to take appropriate risks in any particular situation requires an understanding of two things: the sources and nature of uncertainty, and the degree to which something matters. It is also clear that different things matter to different people to a different extent in different circumstances. As a result, a risk perceived by one person or group as requiring urgent attention may be perceived by others as normal and not worthy of their time. The perception of risk is not an absolute, either present or absent, but is situational and highly dependent on a number of contextual factors. It is this situational aspect of risk that makes the subject of decision-making in uncertain situations both fascinating and important.

Taking appropriate risks requires an underlying understanding of the nature of the challenge. On the one hand, managing risk can be seen as a rational and logical process requiring a grasp of factual historical evidence combined with mathematical assessments of the likelihood of the uncertain event occurring. It is however equally true that managing risk involves the deepest workings of the human brain, as the decisions people make are influenced by a complex interplay of conscious and subconscious factors. This is why one essential component of appropriate risk-taking is an understanding of risk attitude as it applies to individuals and to decision-making groups.

Talking about risk will lead many people to think only about threats, that is, those uncertainties that should they occur would result in an undesirable outcome. However, contemporary management thinking and practice treats risk in a more balanced way. An uncertain set of circumstances could equally lead to positive outcomes, allowing the definition of risk to encompass both opportunities and threats. This double-sided concept of risk is particularly important in the context of effective decision-making, because most decisions need to balance the exploitation or enhancement of hoped-for positive outcomes with the avoidance or mitigation of unwelcome negative ones.

For example, deciding whether to exceed the speed limit when driving a car will depend on a number of uncertainties, including opportunities such as getting to the destination more quickly, and threats such as being arrested or killed during the process. Similarly, deciding whether to seize a business opportunity to launch a new product on to the market before the competition needs to be balanced against the threats to the company's reputation if the new product is not trouble-free. Although each decision is unique, there are no risk-free options. Moreover, zero risk is not only unachievable, it is also undesirable. Failing to take risk would stifle growth and limit improvement. Appropriate risk-taking promotes competitive advantage and stimulates innovation and creativity. Decision-making in a world that is full of 'uncertainty that matters' needs to find an optimal balance of threats and opportunities. The challenge for finding an optimal balance are depicted in Figure 1.1; not too safe, or too unsafe with respect to risks that would mean something bad for objectives, and not too optimistic, or too pessimistic with respect to risks that could create additional value.

Achieving the goal of an optimal balance of threats and opportunities requires a clear understanding of the nature of risk as well as the ability to determine the influence of risk attitude on decision-making.

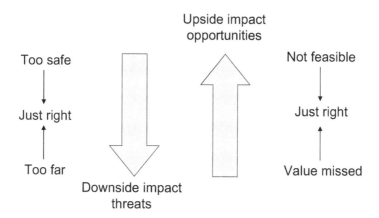

Figure 1.1 Appropriate risk-taking requires optimization of opportunities and threats

Challenges when assessing risk

Risk has two sides: uncertainty, which can be expressed as 'probability' or 'likelihood'; and how much it matters, expressed as 'impact' or 'consequence'. Both of these dimensions need to be understood so that good decisions can be made. If an uncertain event is very unlikely then it might be appropriate to take no explicit action, even though the consequence of that event on objectives would be very significant should it occur. However, different individuals or groups may perceive both likelihood and consequences differently, leading to different decisions.

Take the example of deciding whether to invest time and money in a new business venture, providing coffee for business rail commuters. Of course consumer habits could change for any number of reasons, with a significant beneficial or detrimental effect on coffee sales. However, assessment of the likelihood, nature and scale of any change is largely a matter of perception. Appropriate risk-taking means that people take chances. The degree of effectiveness of that risk-taking depends on how well people understand the chances that they take, and whether they embrace the consequences should the situation turn out differently from their expectations.

If a number of people were faced with the same decision about whether to invest in the business commuters coffee venture, different choices would inevitably be made, driven by the perception by each individual of the underlying risks and the degree to which they mattered. Some people might be highly uncomfortable with the perceived uncertainties and be *averse* to an uncertain outcome; this might lead them to seek certainty even if that meant not pursuing the venture. Others could be quite comfortable with their perception of the uncertainties and *seek* to pursue the venture and take their chances along the way. Another group might be more *tolerant* of the underlying uncertainties, with less strong feelings of comfort or discomfort. Still others could be uncomfortable with ambiguity in the long term so would be prepared to take whatever short-term actions were necessary to deliver a certain long-term outcome: a *neutral* position.

The words 'averse', 'seeking', 'tolerant' or 'neutral' represent a chosen response to uncertainty that matters, driven by perception. This phrase forms a working definition of *risk attitude*, which is a choice made by a given individual or group in the face of a particular risky situation, and which is affected by a range of perceptual factors (these are discussed below).

Labels like risk averse, risk seeking, risk tolerant and risk neutral are useful headlines to describe alternative positions adopted by people when faced with uncertainty. Although labels provide valuable shorthand, their use should not hide the fact that risk attitude exists on a continuous spectrum, as illustrated in Figure 1.2. There are an infinite variety of possible responses to risk which can be displayed by a particular individual or group, but the four basic positions

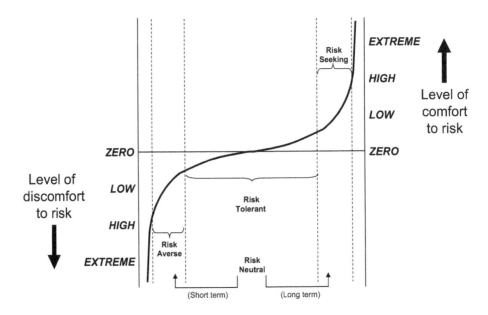

Figure 1.2   Risk attitude spectrum

(adapted from Hillson and Murray-Webster, 2007)

allow a generalized discussion of the topic. These four fundamental risk attitudes are summarized in Table 1.1.

We have explored in other published work how risk attitudes are formed, and concluded that they are usually adopted subconsciously, except when a person or group consciously decides to override their automatic response in order to make a more appropriate choice. Our previous work revealed that the perceptions driving risk attitude are influenced by many factors. These can be grouped under three headings: conscious assessments which are largely rational; subconscious factors including heuristics or mental short-cuts and other sources of cognitive bias; and gut-level affective factors, including feelings and emotions. Table 1.2 provides a composite list of the factors covered by each heading, drawing on the work of various authors, some of whom use different terms to describe the same factor.

Although the various factors affecting perception of risk can be detailed separately under the three headings of conscious, subconscious and affective factors, they do not exist or operate in isolation. They form a triple strand of influence, combining to affect how an individual or a group responds in any given situation, as illustrated in Figure 1.3.

The following paragraphs describe each of three strands in turn. However, while each strand can be teased out separately to aid understanding and explanation, in reality the three are intertwined and each affects the others. There are many cross-links between the different influences on perception, forming a complex web whose effect can be hard to predict.

Table 1.1   Definition of basic risk attitudes

Term	Definition
Risk averse	Uncomfortable with uncertainty, desire to avoid or reduce threats and exploit opportunities to remove uncertainty. Would be unhappy with an uncertain outcome.
Risk seeking	Comfortable with uncertainty, no desire to avoid or reduce threats or to exploit opportunities to remove uncertainty. Would be happy with an uncertain outcome.
Risk tolerant	Tolerant of uncertainty, no strong desire to respond to threats or opportunities in any way. Could tolerate an uncertain outcome if necessary.
Risk neutral	Uncomfortable with uncertainty in the long term so prepared to take whatever short-term actions are necessary to deliver a certain long-term outcome.

Conscious factors (situational and rational)	Subconscious factors	Cognitive bias	Affective factors (emotions and feelings)
	Heuristics		
Familiarity I've/we've done something like this before, or I've/we've never done something like this before	**Intuition** Feels right, I won't look for any more data	**Prospect theory** A bird in the hand is worth two in the bush, double or quits	**Fear (dread, worry, concern...)** Of the consequences of something happening
Manageability I/we know what to do to manage this, or I/we don't know what to do to manage this	**Representativeness** This must be like this other one I've seen before	**Repetition bias** Undue importance is given to repeated data – it must be true!	**Desire (excitement, wonder...)** Of the consequences of something happening
Proximity If it happens it will happen soon so we need to sort it now, or It wouldn't happen for ages, we've got time	**Availability** Most recent data is most memorable. Closely linked to reality traps where 'too much value is attributed to existing situations, blinded by what is, we cannot see what might be if we could disengage from reality'	**Illusion of control** Exaggerate personal influence, discount luck	**Love (lust, adoration, attraction...)** I want it/want more of it
Propinquity If it happens it would really matter to me/us personally, or If it happens it would affect objectives, but it wouldn't really matter to me/us personally	**Confirmation trap** Undue confidence – selective perception: trust me, I'm a ...?	**Illusion of knowledge** Some knowledge or relevant experience masks what isn't known, particularly if the person feels they 'should' know	**Hate (dislike, disgust...)** I don't want it/want less of it
Severity of impact It it happens the effect would be huge (or insignificant)	**Lure of choice** Biased by options that include future alternative judgements – keeping options open	**Intelligence trap** Ability to mentally construct and verbally reason (IQ) means that the conclusions must be correct	**Joy (happy, carefree...)** Life is good, more good things are possible
Group dynamics and organizational culture The norms of how this particular group behaves	**Affect heuristic** Seeking pleasure, avoiding pain	**Optimism bias** Delusional optimism driven by cognitive biases and/or perceived organizational pressures and norms	**Sadness (depressed, morbid...)** Life is bad, more bad things are probable
	Anchoring Attach illogical significance to available data, first impressions last	**Fatalism bias** Ignore probabilities, focus on impact of outcomes – always optimistically, that is, the best case will happen	
	Group effects, e.g. groupthink We all think this way	**Precautionary principle** Ignore probabilities, focus on impact of outcomes – always pessimistically, that is, the worst case will happen	
		Hindsight bias Fail to learn – 'I knew it all along'	

Table 1.2   Summary of potential influences on perception of risk and risk attitude

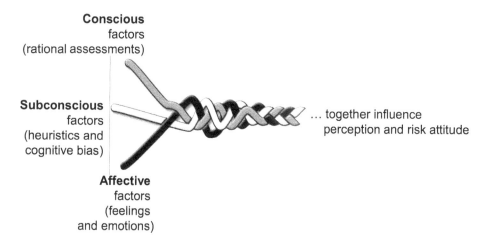

Conscious
factors
(rational assessments)

Subconscious
factors
(heuristics and
cognitive bias)

Affective
factors
(feelings
and emotions)

... together influence
perception and risk attitude

Figure 1.3   The triple strand of influences on perception and risk attitude

Conscious: These factors are based on the visible and measurable characteristics of the situation within which the decision is being made. (Typical conscious factors are listed in Table 1.2.) Such factors are known to bias perceptions of risk for individuals and within groups. They operate in a systematic way, allowing corrections to be made where their influences are exposed. Situational assessments are the most rational part of the triple strand of influences as they tend to be explicit and based on conscious thought.

Subconscious: These factors include mental short-cuts made to facilitate decision-making (heuristics) and other sources of cognitive bias. Heuristics operate at both individual and group levels, and provide mechanisms for making sense of complex or uncertain situations. Based on previous experience, many of these heuristics are useful because they allow rapid filtering of data to determine the most important elements, easing the decision-making task. Unfortunately the fact that heuristics operate subconsciously means that their influence is often hidden, and they can introduce significant bias into decisions. Whereas heuristics can have a positive influence, cognitive biases do not. The effect is to skew perception and decision-making in a way that is not real nor beneficial. Table 1.2 contains common heuristics and sources of cognitive bias that affect both individuals and groups.

Affective: These visceral gut-level responses are based on instinctive emotion or deep underlying feelings rather than rational assessments. All human beings store emotion-charged memories in the limbic system within the brain, and these emotions are automatically triggered in situations perceived to be similar to the stored memory. A wide range of emotions or affective states could influence decision-making (as listed in Table 1.2), although some researchers suggest that the primary influence for any human being is to seek pleasure or to avoid pain.

The triple strand. The three sets of influences which form the triple strand are each important in the context of decision-making, as they each influence perception. Perception drives risk attitude, which in turn affects the quality of decisions made under conditions of uncertainty. It is possible to adopt a reductionist approach when considering these factors, examining the influence of each one in turn. However, the triple strand model has a more important message. The strands do not exist or operate in isolation, but are interwoven to form a complex set of influences. An individual in a decision-making group may have made an apparently rational assessment of the situation and decided on a particular approach, but this assessment will have been shaped by the operation of subconscious heuristics, and coloured by the person's underlying emotions. For example, a person has an opportunity to perform a parachute jump for charity. The person in question thinks that taking part would normally be too risky for them, explaining their decision in terms of a conscious rational assessment of the mathematical probability of injury. They also remember a recent news story where an experienced skydiver died due to a faulty parachute, and this makes them more risk averse, due to the subconscious operation of the availability heuristic. The very thought of jumping out of an aeroplane is enough to make the person's palms sweaty, a sure physiological sign to back up the feeling of dread in their stomach. It's for a good cause (but money could be donated anyway without doing the jump so that could be avoided). The real driving emotion for the person, however, is to avoid being embarrassed (in front of instructors and friends) if they were to 'chicken out' from a jump at the last moment. This adds further emotional weight to the conscious and subconscious perception of the risk. This perception drives their risk attitude (risk averse to the parachute jump) and their ultimate choice not to do it. This assessment is complex enough at an individual level, but would have been more so had there been the influence of a social or work group.

Risk in groups

All of the factors within the triple strand affect the perceptions, risk attitudes and decision-making abilities of both individuals and groups. However, the situation is considerably more complex than simply combining the individual influences to determine their overall effect on the group.

First, individuals are members of multiple groups, as illustrated in Figure 1.4. Every person belongs to a family, though the strength and influence of the family relationship may vary widely. Many individuals have jobs which involve membership of an organization as well as smaller work groups. Most people belong to a local community which in turn exists within a wider national context. Some individuals with the opportunity to travel may even consider themselves to be world citizens.

Each of these levels of membership influences the individual to a greater or lesser extent, and the various groupings also interact. Risk also exists at every level, with interactions between different types of risk.

When applied in the decision-making context, the multiple influences at various group and individual levels present a complex web whose precise effect is hard to determine. It is difficult to rate the relative importance of individual conscious assessments, subconscious heuristics or affective emotions, compared to group dynamics, or societal, organizational and national norms and expectations. These bring a range of influences to bear on individuals, potentially changing their perspectives and risk attitude in a given situation.

It is clear therefore that any complete and meaningful consideration of decision-making in risky situations must address both individuals and groups, and evaluate the effect of this wide range of influences on risk attitudes.

Figure 1.4   Hierarchies of membership and influence (not to scale)

(from Hillson and Murray-Webster. 2007)

Why does understanding risk attitude matter?

No-one would get out of bed in the morning if they had to consciously make a decision about every action to take, so people develop habits and routines that allow their lives to 'free-flow' unless there is an unusual situation to be addressed. The 'free-flow' of individuals and groups is influenced by past experiences and expectations for the future. The perception of uncertainty and the resulting response to out of the ordinary situations is biased by a complex triple strand of intertwined factors including conscious rational assessments, subconscious heuristics and cognitive biases, and gut-level emotions. Each of these three affects both individuals and groups in different ways. The situation is further complicated by various organizational, national or societal influences which impose norms and expectations on individuals and groups.

When decisions have to be made under conditions of uncertainty, each of these influences is important, because they drive the perception of risk. Risk attitude is the chosen response of an individual or group to uncertainty that matters, driven by perception. As a result, the ability to understand risk attitude offers a key to unlock the mysteries of effective decision-making where risk is involved. Understanding risk attitude is a critical success factor which promotes effective decision-making in risky situations, as shown in Figure 1.5.

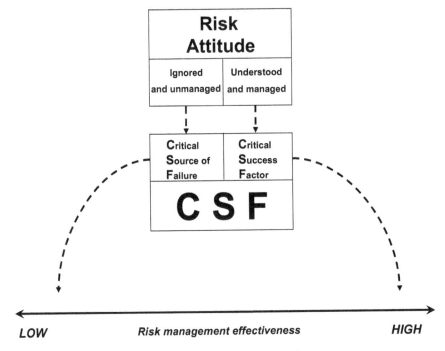

Figure 1.5   Risk attitude as a CSF for effective risk management

However, the absence of this understanding is not neutral, but presents a critical source of failure, leading to reduced effectiveness.

Our previous work (Hillson and Murray-Webster, 2007) presents a thorough analysis of risk attitudes at both individual and group levels. This is recommended for those with a deeper interest in the subject or who need to explore the background concepts in more detail.

Understanding risk attitude is a critical point of departure for effective decision-making, but it is not sufficient; two other parts of the jigsaw need to be put in place. In Chapter 2 we explore the first of these missing pieces, namely to define the notion of a 'good' decision. We summarize the literature on the subject to make the link between risk attitude and decision-making robust.

Second, in order to make a 'good' decision, sometimes risk attitude needs to be intentionally managed to override habitual/normalized patterns of behaviour or to change perspectives that have been biased by erroneous conscious or subconscious influences. Chapter 3 outlines our starting premises about managing risk attitude, particularly to summarize our existing work on individuals and groups, but the story is not complete. The summary in Chapter 3 leads into Part II, where we outline our work to complete the story about understanding and managing risk attitudes for both individuals *and* for groups in pursuit of appropriate risk-taking and optimal decision-making.

What is a Good Decision?

The starting premise for understanding and managing risk attitude is that it matters. One of the main reasons is that effective management of the human influences on risk-taking is essential if good decisions are to be made in uncertain situations. Human beings make decisions in two broad ways: either implicitly and automatically, influenced by hidden or assumed drivers; or explicitly and deliberately, influenced by drivers of which they are more consciously aware. Whichever decision-making route is followed, however, it is not always clear how a 'good' decision might be defined, or even if such a definition is possible. If the role of risk attitudes in decision-making is to be understood and managed, it would be helpful to be able to determine whether or not a decision is good.

There is an extensive body of research related to decision-making in general, and decision-making under uncertainty in particular. This chapter summarizes the key terms and concepts in order to clarify what is meant by a 'good' decision, and to make sense of the link between risk attitude and decision-making.

Principles of decision-making

In its simplest terms, a decision is an allocation of resources (time, money, goodwill) made in order to achieve an objective. The decision-maker is the person or party with control over resource allocation, who decides to make an allocation (or not) depending on their objectives and the values and motives that underpin those objectives.

Every decision situation has three core features:

1. the articulation of the objective or decision to be made (the *framing* of the challenge);

2. the uncertainties that could affect the outcome (the inherent *risks*);

3. the *outcome* itself.

The majority of decisions are made without the aid of specialist decision analysis or models to represent the relationships between these three core features, and this is entirely appropriate and necessary. However, sometimes the decision-maker needs to use more structured tools to compare alternative courses of action and their consequences before deciding what to do.

Clearly, decision-making is more than just the decision itself. Decisions are reached through a process which can be implicit or explicit, simple or complex. As a result, there are two distinct elements to consider when determining whether a decision is 'good' or not, namely:

1.   the quality of the decision-making process adopted;

2.   the effectiveness of the decision outcome in achieving objectives.

These two distinct aspects of decision-making are not necessarily correlated. While people would hope that a good decision-making process would result in a good outcome, this may not be the case. It is entirely possible to have a perfectly good decision-making process which nevertheless results in an unsuccessful outcome. Many people invest in stocks and shares but do not realize a profit. This does not necessarily mean that the original investment decision was poor based on the information available at the time. When an unsuccessful decision outcome arises from a high-quality decision-making process, that is just unlucky.

Conversely, it may be expected that a poor decision-making process would result in a suboptimal outcome, but this may not be the case and a deficient decision-making process can end up with a good outcome. For example, you and your children may arrive safely at your destination after driving down the motorway above the speed limit and with your children unrestrained in the back seat. This successful outcome does not mean that the original decision was good. If a successful decision outcome arises despite a poor decision-making process, it is the result of being lucky.

These two aspects of decision-making – process and outcome – are relevant in all decisions made by all decision-makers, whether individuals or groups, regardless of the complexity of competing objectives, the inherent risks in the situation, or the multiplicity of alternative courses of action that could be adopted. Recognizing these situations should lead towards more truly 'good' decisions, with conscious adoption of an appropriate decision-making process producing a successful decision outcome. The following sections consider the challenges in determining the goodness or quality of the decision-making process and the decision outcome.

The decision-making process

It is easier to define and measure the characteristics of a good process, as opposed to measuring the degree to which a decision outcome is optimal. For example, a good decision-making process is likely to be characterized by most or all of the following:

- the right people are involved;

- all objectives are clearly understood as far as possible;

- uncertainties that could affect achievement of objectives (both damaging threats and beneficial opportunities) are identified, assessed and managed;

- communication processes and values exist that allow perspectives to be shared openly;

- hidden agendas are exposed and dealt with openly;

- differences in perspective that different people bring to the table are explored and valued;

- people are willing to resolve any conflicts in the interests of making the optimal decision;

- data are collected and analyzed as rationally as possible;

- a range of alternatives is considered, not just the obvious one, and alternatives are compared and traded-off against each other.

Research and experience agree that a decision cannot be judged solely by the outcome, but that considerable value can come from improved decision-making processes. Several models exist to define and calibrate the appropriateness of a decision-making process. One of these models, from Strategic Decisions Inc., is described below and is available at http://www.scpd.stanford.edu/scpd/courses/proed/sdrm. It uses the language of quality management to determine whether the decision-making process was fit for purpose in the circumstances.

FEATURES OF A QUALITY OR FIT-FOR-PURPOSE DECISION

This model assesses the quality or 'fitness for purpose' of the decision at the point at which it is being made. It examines six main features of the decision-making process used to get to that point. These are summarized in Table 2.1, and discussed below:

Decision quality criteria
1.   Appropriate frame
2.   Creative, feasible alternatives
3.   Meaningful, reliable information
4.   Clear values and trade-offs
5.   Logically correct reasoning
6.   Commitment to action

Table 2.1   Decision quality criteria
(adapted from Strategic Decisions Inc.)

- The first question is to ask 'Is the decision framed appropriately?' This question addresses whether there is a clear purpose and defined scope that has been agreed upon following discussion. It requires conscious exploration of assumptions, issues, concerns, perspectives and other sources of bias. The decision problem is then phrased in such a way to present the decision-maker with as neutral a choice as possible. A quality decision has a shared perspective of scope and the decisions to be addressed by all the relevant decision-makers and stakeholders.

- The second question asks 'Have a number of creative and valid alternatives been identified that span the solution space?' Most decisions have more than two possible options, but often groups will offer up only one alternative to 'business as usual', missing or ignoring other possibilities. When proposing a number of alternatives there is often no clear winner, but it should be possible to identify the best attributes of each alternative. Work may also be needed to confirm the feasibility of different alternatives. A quality decision chooses the feasible alternative which combines as many of the best attributes from other alternatives as possible.

- Third, 'Has the right amount of appropriate information been gathered to support each alternative?' Meaningful, reliable information makes clear what is important, and is explicit, correct and based on appropriate facts, whilst taking into account all knowable risks (threats and opportunities). A quality decision is linked to a structured risk management process where uncertainty is quantified and the limits of knowledge are known.

- The fourth question to be answered is 'Have clear criteria been established that represent the value being sought by the decision-makers and enable optimal trade-offs to be made?' Wants and needs are discussed and translated into clear attributes that represent success. This involves engaging stakeholders, understanding their value drivers, and being explicit about important preferences and expectations as far as possible. A quality decision has clear and explicit attributes, and the relevant priority between these attributes is articulated allowing trade-offs to be made.

- Fifth, 'Is the logic underpinning the decision clear and correct?' This question examines links and dependencies so that models can be created with explicit logic. This assumes that logically correct reasoning cannot exist if decision-makers rely on single-point, deterministic information instead of using a probabilistic approach. Deterministic thinking is common in Western societies, with the conviction that there is 'one right answer'. This leads to rejection of possible optimal solutions. Probabilistic approaches, supported by simulation models, can address multiple possible outcomes based on source data, allowing more feasible options to be considered. Accordingly a quality decision has clear, explicit, correct logic where dependencies are clearly mapped and probabilistic analysis has been performed.

- Finally, the test of a quality decision asks 'Is there commitment to action from key players?' Lack of active interest by key decision-makers is likely to lead to insurmountable organizational hurdles. Active participation is needed by the right people. For a quality decision to exist, there needs to be buy-in and commitment to action from the decision-makers as well as the teams that are required to implement the decision.

Decision-making groups can take each of these six questions in turn and decide the degree to which the decision-making process has satisfied the criteria. Results can be plotted on a simple radar plot (as illustrated in Figure 2.1), to determine whether the process has been appropriate. The aim is not to meet all six criteria perfectly, but any weaknesses exposed by this analysis can be addressed to strengthen the decision-making process in future.

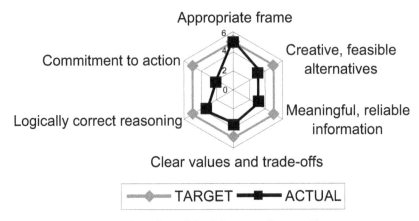

Figure 2.1   Example radar plot of decision quality attributes

Decision outcomes

It is relatively easy to assess the quality of a decision-making process: the position is less clear when it comes to decision outcomes. It is natural to want to know whether there is an absolute 'right answer' for any given decision situation, but this presents a number of challenges.

In theory most problems have a mathematically optimal answer. However, decisions are very complex, given the levels of uncertainty that are inherent in most situations and the mix of rational data and less rational assumptions and guesses which influence the outcome. As a result, in practice it is not likely to be possible to determine an absolute right answer for most decisions.

The challenges in determining the quality of a particular decision outcome arise from three types of decision problem:

1.   dilemmas

2.   paradoxes

3.   difficult decisions.

These three challenges are not equally distributed in most business, the majority being just difficult. However, it is important to understand the other two types, as they may occasionally arise and cause decision-making problems.

DILEMMA

A dilemma can be defined as 'a situation requiring a choice between equally undesirable (or desirable) alternatives'. Consequently dilemmas appear to be insoluble, with no right answer. Fortunately most real-world decisions are not true dilemmas, although they do sometimes occur, and the skilled decision-maker must be able to recognize them and act accordingly. Where dilemmas arise in reality, they can often be addressed by considering the effect of cooperation or non-cooperation on decision outcomes.

The dilemma is well known in logic theory, particularly in the field of applied mathematics and economics known as game theory. The best-known dilemma is perhaps the so-called 'Prisoner's Dilemma', which represents a class of situations where it is not possible to calculate the best outcome for all parties.

A business example may be when contractors are bidding competitively but without knowledge of each other's bids. Without talking to the other bidder, each contractor must decide in isolation, based on their values and drivers to win the work. They would inevitably also try to second guess the decisions and actions of the other bidder and the client. This may lead to a change in their decision, although it still does not allow them to predict the decision outcome.

PARADOX

A paradox is a self-contradictory or counter-intuitive statement or argument: it is logically impossible and cannot be solved with a single correct outcome. For example the statement 'I am always a liar' is paradoxical, since if the statement is true then it is also a lie. Another common paradox is the assertion that 'there are no absolutes', which itself is an absolute. Paradoxes are also sometimes presented as a pair of propositions both of which seem logical but which are mutually exclusive. A common procurement example might be where a purchaser tells potential contractors that they will select the lowest bidder who meets the full specification, but also ask bidders to propose costed scope changes. The bid price can be reduced by reducing scope, but this reduces the chance of being selected against other bidders who offer to meet the full specification.

As for dilemmas, paradoxical decision situations are not the norm in real life, but they occasionally happen and need to be managed. They can often be eliminated by clarification of language and terms, as well as definition of unambiguous decision criteria.

DIFFICULT

The third category of challenging decision situation arises because some decisions are just difficult. There can be many causes for this. For example, in many situations a right answer could be theoretically possible, but the constraints of time and/or resource availability lead to short-cuts in the decision-making process and drive the decision-makers to make compromises and judgements without having all the salient data to hand.

In addition, many decisions are difficult due to the complex influences of a number of competing factors: in particular, human factors make most decisions more complex than they would otherwise be. These human factors include perceptions of risk and attitudes towards them, which is why understanding and managing risk attitudes is essential to good decision-making.

Seminal research into decision bias

The discussion above shows that while it is theoretically possible for there to be such a thing as an absolute 'good' or 'appropriate' decision outcome, in practice decision-makers are unlikely to be able to determine what this might be, either due to the existence of true dilemma or paradox, or due to inherent difficulties in the decision-making situation. As a result, it is easier to determine whether or not a decision is 'good' by considering the decision-making process rather than the outcome. It is of course possible to deal rationally with different aspects of the decision-making process, but there are many influences on risk attitude and decision-making that are *not* rational because they are related to human perceptions, values and biases.

Chapter 1 summarized those factors that bias perception for individuals and groups (see Table 1.2). Any of these factors may also be sources of bias for a decision-making group in a particular situation. The area of decision bias however is more complex than just the perceptual factors influencing individuals and groups, as demonstrated in seminal research into Prospect Theory by Kahnemann and Tversky (1979).

Prospect Theory challenges Bernoulli's Expected Utility Theory, published in 1738. Bernoulli suggested that decision-making by human beings is linked to the value of an item measured not by price, but by the utility (usefulness) it provides to the owner. A rational person will try to maximize their utility in decision choices. Kahnemann and Tversky discovered that the utility attributed to an item decreases in inverse proportion to the amount of gain already made, or increases in inverse proportion to the amount of loss already suffered. In simpler terms, people tend to become more cautious or risk averse to taking a further chancy decision as they gain more, and perhaps counter-intuitively, they become more risk seeking as they lose more. This is reflected by common proverbs such as 'A bird in the hand is worth two in the bush', or 'Quit while you're ahead' (risk aversion varies in inverse proportion to gains); 'You may as well be hung for a sheep as for a lamb' or 'Double or nothing' (risk seeking varies in inverse proportion to losses). These results would not be predicted by pure Expected Utility Theory.

Kahnemann and Tversky's work is most famously represented by the asymmetrical utility curve, as shown in Figure 2.2.

A further key discovery by Kahnemann and Tversky relates to the framing (description) of the decision problem. Here, in experiments where people had to decide between 'definitely saving lives', or taking the chance to 'prevent people from dying' there was clear evidence that human beings, rather than being risk averse, are actually 'loss-averse'. In experiments where rationally there was no difference in the statements made (the gain or loss were the same actual value), the majority of respondents would play safe regarding a gain, but would go to absurd lengths to avoid a loss.

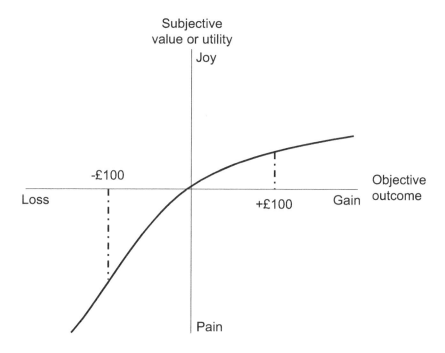

Figure 2.2   Gains and losses not of equal value

(Prospect Theory *from Kahnemann and Tversky, 1979*)

The choice below illustrates the influence of framing:

> *The UK is preparing for an outbreak of a novel disease that is expected to kill 600 people. Two treatment programmes have been proposed, with exact scientific estimates of the results.*
>
> - *If Programme 1 is adopted, 200 people will be saved.*
>
> - *If Programme 2 is adopted, there is a one-third probability that 600 people will be saved and a two-thirds probability that no people will be saved.*
>
> *Which programme would you select?*

Both programmes have the same statistical expected value, but most people favour Programme 2 because it explicitly states the possibility that everyone might die.

Related work indicated that people are very poor at assessing probabilities reliably. For example, most people answer Yes to the question 'Would you take up a new sport if it increased your annual chances of death from 1 in 10 000 to 1.3 in 10 000?' On the other hand, most people answer No if asked 'Would you take up a new sport if it resulted in a 30 per cent increase in your annual chance of death?'

Kahnemann and Tversky's research findings caused huge interest when published, particularly in economics, as they virtually destroyed the notion of the rational decision made by the informed and rational decision-maker. They also severely challenged the validity of decisions made using 'intuition' by experienced people in an uncertain environment. The findings opened the door for a much more person-centred approach to decision-making, and one that took the research out of the lab-based environment and away from experiments using games of pure chance and into the real world of complex decisions made by groups of individuals all with differing perspectives, drivers and thought processes. Although the work of Kahnemann and Tversky addresses only some of the biases on human perception of risk, they are generally appreciated as being significant.

Other influences

In summarizing the vast amount of research into the subject of decision-making under uncertainty, there are two other areas that must be mentioned: the influence of personality traits on decision-making and the role of experience.

PERSONALITY TRAITS

There is a wide body of research that focuses on the personality traits of individuals and their influence on individual and group decision-making processes. Such research demonstrates the way in which individuals naturally seek to move decision-making processes and actual decisions into their 'frame of reference and comfort zone'.

Based on such research, it is clear that personality-based preferences of influential stakeholders might influence overall group dynamics. Recognizing this, overall decision quality can be considered in the context of the personality traits of decision-makers. Instruments such as the Myers-Briggs Type Indicator (MBTI™) or the Spony Profiling Model provide useful frameworks for this type of assessment.

Both MBTI and Spony Profiling Model are derived from Jungian psychology, which asserts that human beings value some modes of thinking and acting over others, and that the preferred styles have dominance in terms of expressed behaviour. The two models assess people across a number of scales, as shown in Figure 2.3.

Those personality traits that have a direct impact on risk attitudes and decision-making preferences need to be understood if individuals are to be

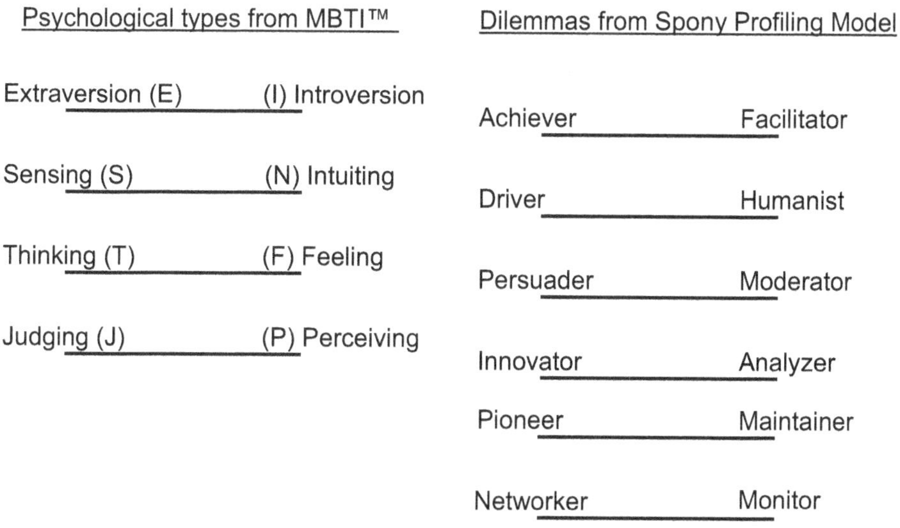

Psychological types from MBTI™   Dilemmas from Spony Profiling Model

Extraversion (E)   (I) Introversion
                                           Achiever   Facilitator

Sensing (S)   (N) Intuiting
                                           Driver   Humanist

Thinking (T)   (F) Feeling
                                           Persuader   Moderator

Judging (J)   (P) Perceiving
                                           Innovator   Analyzer

                                           Pioneer   Maintainer

                                           Networker   Monitor

Figure 2.3   **Personality traits that influence preferences for decision-making**

effective decision-makers as part of a wider group. For example, one person's preference may be to process information and make decisions using a 'thinking' frame of reference that makes decisions based on defined criteria using strong logic and causality. Such a person might not understand another's inclination for using a 'feeling' frame of reference that makes decisions based on a deep understanding of value drivers and personal criteria. This is reflected in the Myers Briggs T–F dimension. The J–P dimension is often associated with risk attitude, where the J preference values have a firm plan of action with risks identified and managed wherever possible (risk averse). Conversely the P preference is to 'keep options open' and take advantage of emerging changes, which is more closely associated with risk seeking behaviour.

In another case, one person may prefer to make decisions independently, quickly and spontaneously, unfettered by the views of other people. Such a person might not understand another's desire for following a structured and methodical process, consulting others and taking time to consider alternatives and options. The two Spony dilemmas, Pioneer–Maintainer and Innovator–Analyzer, address this situation. In particular, the Pioneer preference values risk seeking attributes whereas the Maintainer prefers risk averse, cautious behaviour.

EXPERIENCE

Decision-scientist and researcher Gary Klein has written extensively about the decision-making processes used by highly experienced people when making decisions alone. He used anthropological research methods to study fire-fighters at close quarters, and observed that very experienced people do not follow rational, methodical decision-analysis processes (for example, defining and assessing a number of alternatives then choosing one). Instead they rely heavily on intuitive processes. In retrospect such people recognize that they did not consciously make the decision, but were able to justify their decision in terms of historical experience of similar situations.

Klein's analysis provides key insights into these decision-making situations, but suffers from two shortcomings when applied to group decision-making under conditions of uncertainty. First, it considers only the experience of a single practitioner, and second there appears to be no explicit step to evaluate the 'quality' of the decision before taking it. These shortcomings are directly relevant to group decision-making. Very experienced people have a tendency to 'know' the right answer using intuitive processes, but are often faced with the challenges of explaining how they made their decisions and bringing their colleagues along with them.

Conscious competence

Chapter 1 established that understanding risk attitudes is important so that inappropriate attitudes are not adopted which might lead us away from making good decisions. This chapter has explored further the notion of a 'good' decision and concluded that performance can best be improved by focusing on decision-making processes, making them as robust and understood as possible. Doing this inevitably means addressing explicitly the drivers behind the attitudes to the risks inherent in any particular decision.

All this indicates that to improve our decision-making we need to bring to the surface those values, preferences, attitudes and behaviours that are held unconsciously, and make ourselves consciously aware of them so they can be examined and modified if that is what we choose.

This process of uncovering can be usefully explored using the 'conscious competence learning matrix' model. This has been attributed by some to Noel Burch (1970s) who seems to be responsible for defining the language within the model. Others recognize William C Howell (1977) as creator of the model in its most used form, as shown in Figure 2.4. The conscious competence learning matrix has two dimensions: consciousness (or awareness), and competence (or ability). Each dimension can be either present or absent. This provides a four-step generic model that generates valuable insights into a range of situations, and is most frequently applied to the learning cycle.

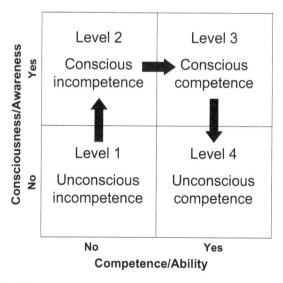

Figure 2.4 **The Conscious Competence Learning Matrix**
(adapted from Howell, 1977)

The first level is termed unconscious incompetence, where we are unaware of our inability, with blind spots, not knowing what we don't know. In order to progress it is first necessary to expose this inadequacy, moving to Level 2, conscious incompetence. Here we recognize our areas of weakness and deficiency, becoming aware of where we lack the necessary ability. From this position it is possible to take steps to address any shortcomings, learning to perform the required skills. This usually needs concentration and focus, to ensure that the newly acquired skills are used properly, and this stage is termed conscious competence. The model includes a further level, where the learned skills or abilities become natural and can be performed without conscious attention, which is called unconscious competence.

The conscious competence learning matrix can clearly be applied to decision-making, which is a learned skill that can be develop and improved. However, many people regard their decision-making ability as second nature and few have examined the extent of their competence in this skill. This would obviously be valuable, in order to make people aware of their level of decision-making ability, both individually and in groups, and to lead to better decision processes and outcomes. However, in the context of decision-making, it is questionable whether Level 4 in the conscious competence learning matrix is desirable as the final position to which people should aspire. There are clear dangers in assuming that one possesses unconscious competence, able to make good decisions without use of an examined process. Without application of conscious examination it would be possible to drift unknowingly from Level 4 to Level 1, losing competence without being aware of it. This suggests that a regular revisiting of Level 3 might be valuable, consciously checking one's abilities to ensure that one remains competent.

Some commentators on the conscious competence learning matrix (for example Dychoff, 2007) take a different approach to addressing the dangers that can arise when a skill has been habitualized. Instead of recommending a return to Level 3, they have introduced a fifth level into the model – chosen conscious competence. This is required when 'elements of what we do are so critical to successful performance that the highest level of learning is to choose to remain consciously competent'. This situation applies to decision-making in situations that are uncertain and where the outcome matters. It is unwise for individuals and groups in such situations to rely on (assumed) unconscious competence when making important decisions. Instead they should ensure that competence is maintained by regular intentional examination, followed by corrective or developmental action where necessary.

Table 2.2 expands the standard conscious competence learning matrix model to include chosen conscious competence. For each of the five levels, the table summarizes the degree of awareness and competence, and comments on development actions that might be appropriate to move to the next level and ultimately to achieve Level 5, chosen conscious competence.

While the standard conscious competence learning model can be applied to the skill of decision-making, its extension to the fifth level is particularly relevant. Many individuals and groups aspire to unconscious competence in decision-making, seeking the ability to make good decisions intuitively. We have seen however that this position holds dangers. Decision-making ability can be eroded by complacency, thinking that there is no need to maintain the skill since it is just second nature for the person or group to make good decisions.

Table 2.2   Steps to building chosen conscious competence

Level	Awareness	Competence	Development action
Level 1 **Unconscious incompetence**	Not aware of the existence or relevance of the skill, or of their deficiency in it	Unable to perform the skill, and does not attempt it	Become conscious of the need for the skill and their inability to perform it
Level 2 **Conscious incompetence**	Aware of the existence and relevance of the skill, recognizes their limited ability, and realizes that developing their skill will improve effectiveness	Unable to perform the skill without active assistance from others	Understand the size and importance of the gap, and be committed to bridging it through training, mentoring, experience etc.
Level 3 **Conscious competence**	Aware of the need to concentrate and focus on the skill in order to perform it reliably	Can perform reliably, at will and without assistance, and able to demonstrate and explain to others	Continue to practice the skill in various application areas, to consolidate and maintain ability
Level 4 **Unconscious competence**	Not aware of their ability to perform the skill, done as 'second nature'	Performs reliably, although may find it difficult to explain what has become largely instinctive to them	Recognize own abilities, consciously consider how they were obtained and how they can be maintained
Level 5 **Chosen conscious competence**	Aware of the existence and relevance of the skill, and of their current level of performance	Performs reliably and can teach others easily, understanding the drivers of competence	Maintain and enhance current skill level through regular refresher activities and comparison against best practice

It is also possible for the skills of the unconsciously competent individual or group to become outdated as new techniques and challenges arise.

As a result, the fifth level in the model, chosen conscious competence, is the required destination for individuals or groups who wish to make good decisions. This is also the place where risk attitudes can be examined consciously, to become aware of their role in the decision-making process, with the objective of making better quality decisions.

Conclusion

The previous chapter explored our current *understanding* of risk attitudes, and in this chapter we made an explicit link between risk attitudes and decision-making. The next chapter takes us from understanding to *managing*, summarizing what is currently known about how to manage risk attitude. Work in this area to date has largely concentrated on individuals, leaving relatively uncharted the topic of managing group risk attitude, which is addressed in the rest of this book.

Managing Risk Attitude

Although understanding risk attitude is a critical point of departure for ensuring an effective decision-making process, it is not sufficient. Sometimes the risk attitudes adopted by individuals and groups need to be managed intentionally. This enables patterns of behaviour which have become habitual or normalized to be challenged and modified as necessary. It also helps change perspectives that have been biased by erroneous conscious or subconscious influences. This chapter summarizes existing work regarding the management of risk attitudes, outlining the prerequisites for any individual or group who want to make a change that will lead to more appropriate risk-taking and decision-making.

Prerequisites for managing risk attitude

There are a number of foundational concepts and frameworks that provide key insights into the subject of risk attitudes. Each of these is useful in its own right, but incomplete as a framework to manage risk attitudes. We have explored each of these concepts and frameworks in other work, but the main ideas are outlined here as a basis for what follows.

Three core concepts that underpin the perception and management of risk attitudes are the Triune Brain as described by Paul MacLean (1974), Transactional Analysis (Berne 1961), and the Mindset of Choice.

1. The Triune Brain presents a three-level model of the human brain that explains the difference between instinctive behaviour (originating from the brainstem), emotion-laden memories (stored in the limbic system), and rational thought (centred in the neocortex). The human brain 'filters' all information through the limbic system which means that no situation is ever interpreted entirely rationally; emotions are always at play when human beings make decisions.

2. Transactional Analysis explains how perceptions of self and others lead to different external behaviours. Behaviours that are underpinned by an 'I'm OK, You're OK' mindset and expressed from the 'adult' ego-state are more rational that those expressed from other states, e.g. 'I'm OK, You're not OK' from the parent or child.

3. Mindset of Choice emphasizes the importance of active choosing of attitudes towards any given situation, as opposed to reactive or driven positions. With choice comes consequence. The Mindset of Choice chooses to choose, and is accountable for the outcomes arising from that choice. It is a mature life position based on free will; a notion underpinned by the vast majority of the world's religious and philosophical teachings.

While these three core concepts provide a rich set of insights into human behaviour they are necessarily general in their application, and do not provide the whole picture with regard to the management of risk attitudes. The field of emotional literacy is more specific. Emotional literacy examines how individuals can address their feelings, drivers and emotions proactively, and there are several models in the literature. These can be consolidated into four basic steps, summarized as:

1. recognize emotions

2. understand emotions

3. appropriately express emotions

4. handle emotions.

Each of these steps can be further subdivided into constituent elements, allowing detailed analysis of the contributors to emotional literacy in a given situation.

Emotional literacy is usually applied to the management of emotions and feelings. It does however offer a powerful framework for understanding and managing risk attitudes for both individuals and groups. While the relevance of emotional literacy to the affective thread of the triple strand model is clear, in fact the techniques and approaches embodied in emotional literacy can be more widely applied to both conscious and subconscious elements.

In addition, the standard emotional literacy approach mainly concerns individuals, though additional factors applying to groups have been identified.

These are mainly related to leadership characteristics, since the relationship between individuals and groups is most clearly seen in the way leaders operate. Leadership is a very wide topic: only certain aspects are relevant to the management of risk attitudes, and even these do not address the whole area. Nevertheless it is clear that emotionally intelligent leadership is a key prerequisite for managing risk attitudes in groups.

So we can draw upon useful insights from the three core concepts of Triune Brain, Transactional Analysis and Mindset of Choice, as well as the emotional literacy framework for individuals and its extension to groups. While neither the core concepts nor emotional literacy are completely fit for this purpose in isolation, it is possible to synthesize them into a single rationalized framework, as shown in Table 3.1. This maps the core concepts and the component parts of the emotional literacy model, and groups them under four generic headings, which we can call the 'Four A's':

1. Awareness of self and others;

2. Appreciation of self and others;

3. Assertion of needs and issues;

4. Action to achieve goals and intentions.

The left-hand column of Table 3.1 indicates that the three core concepts of Triune Brain, Transactional Analysis and Mindset of Choice map broadly to awareness, appreciation and action respectively. More detailed mapping is presented in the other two columns of Table 3.1. The middle column presents emotional literacy for individuals, which is typically focused on understanding and management of emotions, and shows how its elements map into the Four A's. Similarly, the right-hand column takes those leadership factors in emotional literacy for groups which are required in addition to the individual emotional literacy elements, and maps those to the Four A's.

The Four A's offer a useful summary of the key factors to consider when seeking to manage risk attitudes, combining the best of the three core concepts with the insights of applied emotional literacy. They offer rationalization of a large number of constituent parts which is simple without being simplistic. The four steps can then be applied across all three triple strand elements, namely conscious, subconscious and affective factors, to manage risk attitude where that is judged to be necessary to meeting objectives.

Table 3.1   Mapping to the Four A's

Core concepts	Emotional literacy for individuals	Emotional literacy for groups
A. Triune Brain [1]	A. Recognize emotions: • Self-awareness [1] • Organizational awareness [1] • Empathy [2] • Trust [2]	Cultural fluency [2]
		Objective-setting [3]
B. Transactional Analysis [2]	B. Understand emotions: • Relative regard [2] • Flexibility/adaptability [2] • Personal power/self-confidence [2/3]	Use of power [3]
	C. Express emotions appropriately: • Goal-directedness [3] • Personal openness/ emotional honesty [3]	Use of language [3]
C. Mindset of Choice [3]	• Assertiveness [3] • Conflict handling [3] • Optimism [3] • Constructive discontent [3]	Meeting behaviours [3/4]
	D. Handle emotions: • Intentionality [4] • Resilience [4] • Interdependence [4]	Group motivation [4]

Key: [1] = Awareness; [2] = Appreciation; [3] = Assertion; [4] = Action.

This summary of the existing work on factors influencing risk attitudes shows the complexity of the field. There are many overlapping and interrelated influences, each of which exerts a distinct effect on risk attitude, but is also modified by the other factors. The task of dissecting the various influences is not trivial, and requires care and attention. As with all complex challenges, accurate diagnosis of the situation is the first step towards dealing with it effectively.

So how do the four areas of awareness, appreciation, assertion and action relate to managed risk attitude that results in appropriate risk-taking and quality decision-making? This can perhaps best be illustrated through a fictional example. The following text tells a story based on real-life experience to which the reader should be able to relate without too much difficulty. As the narrative unfolds, various aspects of the Four A's are revealed, and the reader is invited to identify how these operate in influencing the risk attitudes displayed by the various players in the story. Most of the factors in Table 3.1 are demonstrated in the story. Appendix A indicates the links.

From Brazil to Bulgaria?

Export Excellence Limited is a British company with headquarters, research and development and manufacturing based in England. Last year the company succeeded in expanding their product offering into South America, which was a new geographic market for them. The Chief Executive Officer, buoyed by this recent success, intends to press ahead and conquer another market, this time in Eastern Europe. He has called a meeting of the senior management team (SMT) to discuss this opportunity. The story is told from the perspective of Paul, who is personal assistant to the CEO, and who took the minutes of the management meeting.

Paul arrived home to find his wife Wendy growing increasingly impatient. 'You're late for dinner. Where have you been?' she demanded. 'Sorry darling, the SMT meeting ran over – again,' he replied wearily. 'Typical senior managers, always letting their emotions get in the way of a simple decision.' 'I suppose you're going to tell me all about it,' she sighed. 'Well if you don't mind, and you might even find it interesting. It all started when Theo our CEO told us his plans to launch our new product in Eastern Europe.' Paul's mind wandered back to the boardroom…

> 'Right everyone, settle down,' said Theo. 'No time for small-talk, we've got business to do. I hope you're all ready to make some good decisions this afternoon?' Theo gave a short confident laugh, clearly relishing the prospect of what was to come. He obviously didn't realize how his apparent self-confidence annoyed some of his colleagues. His PA Paul, who knew most of the management team quite well, looked down at his laptop, seeming to concentrate on taking the minutes, but trying to work out in his mind who would be the first to speak their mind and challenge the boss. He didn't have long to wait.

> 'Good decisions?' muttered Fiona. 'You mean doing what we're told, more like.' 'What?' said Theo. 'Is that a valuable contribution from our esteemed Finance Department?' 'Nothing,' Fiona replied, 'just ignore me,' adding under her breath, '… as usual.'

> 'OK, let me set the scene.' Theo was enjoying himself. 'As you all know, our recent expansion into South America was fantastic. The Megatronic range was a runaway success, beyond most of our wildest dreams – well I always thought it would go well, despite some negativity from the usual quarters.' A quick glance at Fiona left no doubt who he meant. 'First-year sales have exceeded our target by 20 per cent, margin is higher than expected due to aggressive local sourcing agreements, and there's a healthy outlook for continued growth into the foreseeable

future. Our agent in Brazilia says she's never seen such take up of an imported product. I knew it would work, so well done to all of you who worked hard to back me on this one.'

'Just lucky I reckon,' Fiona whispered to Owen the Operations Director, who seemed to be listening closely to Theo, and quietly nodding his apparent agreement. 'Shhh,' he said, 'I'm trying to see where this is going.'

'Anyway, since our South American launch was so successful, I think we should build on our momentum, strike while the iron's hot, maintain our first-mover advantage, and take Megatronic into another new market. Everyone at the golf club is talking about Eastern Europe as the hot place to be, and my cousin's just bought a villa outside Sofia, so I thought Bulgaria would be as good a place as any. What do you think? Any objections?'

Paul held his breath, waiting for Fiona to make her move. He was surprised that Owen spoke first. 'First of all, congratulations on the Brazil success,' he started. 'I wasn't sure it would work at first, given our lack of experience in South America. There's no doubt Megatronic has hit the market and is doing well for us there. Mind you I'm run off my feet making sure that our ops set-up can meet the unexpected high demand. But I must admit I've got a few concerns about what to do next. Bulgaria isn't Brazil, and we ought to be careful before we rush into something that we can't sustain. From an operations point of view there are lots of things we'd need to know first before we could make a proper decision.'

Theo was quick to react. 'No, we've got a strategy that works, we proved that in Brazil. All we need to do is be bold, and do it again. I'm sure it will be fine. I've thought about this a lot, and if we hesitate we'll lose the chance. It feels right somehow, and I don't want to wait.'

Owen was just about to reply, but Fiona's voice was harsh as she cut across him. 'Come on, you can't be serious Theo. I know we've been lucky once, but we can't bet the company's future on another unknown market. What do you know about Bulgaria? Where's the costed launch plan? Who are our in-country agents? What about regulations and local practices? There are too many variables – we've got to do a full risk assessment before we can even think about deciding on this. As Finance Director I could never agree to such a risky venture without knowing what's at stake. We can't just assume that our luck will hold second time around.'

'I knew you'd react like this – it's a typical negative reaction from Finance. You bean-counters are always over-cautious. We don't have time for a risk assessment, and anyway it only tells us what we already know, that bad stuff happens but the bold win the prize.' Paul wondered whether he should minute the fact that Theo had turned red and seemed to be getting warm. Then he glanced at Fiona and saw her eyes flash with anger. This could get interesting, he thought.

Wendy interrupted him with a question. 'I hope you're not about to imply that Fiona was getting emotional just because she's a woman?' 'Of course not darling,' Paul said quickly, 'and there's no need for you to get upset.' Wendy laughed, recognizing the gentle irony, and kicked her husband gently under the table. 'There's nothing wrong with emotions. But did you say anything?' she asked. 'I'd have been tempted to get involved.' 'I wish you'd been there, you'd have brought a bit of common sense,' Paul replied. 'But I'm just the PA taking minutes, no-one wants my opinion. All I do is write down what happens. So my notes say "Following the Megatronic launch in Brazil, possible expansion into Bulgaria was proposed. There was a frank exchange of views. Conducting a risk assessment was discussed but rejected." 'Very diplomatic,' smiled Wendy, 'perhaps you should be Chief Exec.' 'One day maybe,' said Paul. 'But I won't be like Theo, that's for sure. Anyway you'll never guess what happened next… Just when it seemed that things would turn nasty, with all-out confrontation between Theo and Fiona, Owen surprised us all.'

'Can I make a suggestion Theo?' Owen spoke louder than usual, sitting forward in his chair and looking straight at the CEO. Everyone turned their attention towards him. The mild-mannered Operations Director seemed about to do something totally out of character. 'It's obvious that there are a number of ways of looking at this situation, and different people will have different views on how best to proceed. You and Fiona are probably both right. It's a great opportunity for us to explore another market, now that we know from Brazil that Megatronic sells outside UK. Clearly we can't just ignore those facts. But it's also true that Bulgaria is an unknown quantity and there's lots we don't know about doing business there. I think we need a period of reflection to consider our options, rather than jumping to a decision today. We ought to focus on the situation and not get personal. It's probably also a good idea to get someone neutral involved who can make an unbiased assessment of the situation and give us some well-defined recommendations. I propose

a short focused study, identifying the lessons we can learn from Brazil, laying out what needs to be done in Bulgaria, and then we can decide where to go from there. What do you think?'

Theo took a deep breath. The truth was that he really wanted to get started in Bulgaria, if only to prove to the others that Brazil hadn't been pure luck. He was getting frustrated with his team's unwillingness to get on with it. He'd always expected opposition from Fiona, who seemed to see the downside in everything. However, Owen was right, there was a lot they didn't know about Eastern Europe, and the 'neutral study' offered a face-saving way out of confrontation with Fiona. There was just one problem…

'OK, but who's going to do the study? I'm sure you don't want me to lead it, as I already know the right answer. I can also tell you now what Fiona would say. You're too busy Owen taking care of the Brazil situation, and I can't spare you for this. Any ideas?'

The room went quiet as the senior management team considered the options. Who understood the issues, was familiar with the business, and could be trusted by everyone to be impartial? Eventually they all reached the same conclusion, and all eyes turned to…

'You're not serious?' said Wendy. 'I said you might find it interesting!' Paul replied. 'My initial reaction was "Who, me? Surely not, I'm just the humble PA who takes the minutes" – but it seems not. The SMT have asked me to spend a week looking at how to take the Megatronic product range to Eastern Europe. I've got to think about the threats and opportunities we face, try to work out which are most important, and make sensible suggestions on how they might be handled. Actually I'm quite looking forward to it.'

'But what about Theo and Fiona? Won't you just end up stuck in the middle, caught in the crossfire when they take your study and use it to support their preconceived ideas? It seems like you're taking some personal risk here. Are you sure you want to do this?'

'Well no risk, no reward,' smiled Paul. 'Of course I'll need to think hard about how I present my conclusions. I'll probably need to chat to all the key players beforehand to get their buy-in. I'll have to separate the issues from the personalities as far as possible. And I'm sure I can find a way to keep both the CEO and Finance onside, even if I have to be a bit assertive – you can help me with that part! And who knows, if I get this right it could be very good for my career. How do you fancy moving to Sofia?'

Summary

Every human being adopts attitudes towards the risks they perceive; these attitudes then drive behaviour. Sometimes risk attitudes lead us away from, rather than towards, appropriate risk-taking and good decision-making.

Self-awareness is central to knowing when this may be happening, and to exposing the sources of bias that are leading to erroneous perception of and behaviour towards risk. For individuals to take appropriate risks, they need to be aware of the conscious assessments, subconscious biases and affective influences that are shaping their perceptions. When it is a group rather than an individual making decisions in uncertain situations, awareness and appreciation of the views and perceptions of the other parties is also critical. Trust, empathy and respect for different perceptions and cross-cultural influences underpin relative regard, leading to the mindset that believes that 'I'm OK, You're OK'.

Often there are situations where risk attitudes lead to inappropriate risk-taking, but where the stakes are not high and conscious management of the erroneous risk attitude is not considered a priority. When however it does matter, as with decisions leading to any significant change, people can choose whether and how to assert their needs and articulate the issues they perceive. This choice undoubtedly poses additional personal risk in some circumstances, but crossing the verbal barrier is a prerequisite for management of any personal change. Finally, action is required in order to see through the plan, often needing intentionality (delayed gratification), optimism and resilience in the face of pressure.

Emotional literacy is the key to managing attitudes to risk. This is difficult enough to do when only one person is involved, but it is possible with intent. It is much more difficult when more people are involved and where there are undoubtedly more influences and greater complexity.

Some insights into managing group risk attitude have already been raised in our earlier work, but much more needs to be understood in order to develop a framework to enable groups of people to manage their adopted risk attitude in situations that matter, leading to more effective decision-making.

In Part I, we re-stated and elaborated our previous understanding of risk attitudes, how they are formed and their influence on decision-making. We have also summarized an approach to the management of risk attitude using applied emotional literacy. This work, which is largely complete for the management of individual risk attitudes, is incomplete when it comes to group risk attitude.

In Part II we will turn exclusively to groups and to the task of unpicking the numerous variables that influence the formation of risk attitude. Our aim is to find a coherent framework for effective management of risk attitudes in groups, especially when they are making decisions perceived to be both risky and important. Part III then explains the practical steps involved in the active management of group risk attitude in such decision-making situations.

PART II

Group Risk Attitude in Action: From Theory to Practice

Drivers of Group Risk Attitude   CHAPTER

4

A lot has been written about decision-making under conditions of uncertainty, and there is a large body of knowledge describing the various sources of bias which influence such decisions. Our summary of this work in Chapter 2 indicates that much of the work carried out has been academic in nature, undertaken by research groups in non-natural settings, with artificial constraints. Often the subjects are students or volunteers, and decision situations are engineered to provide usable data or to answer very specific questions as part of strictly scientific research. Such research aims to advance theoretical understanding and is robust enough to withstand debate and scrutiny; however it is not so good for addressing practical application, because the necessarily artificial laboratory setting fails to separate and test the interplay between the large number of real-life variables.

Academic research into psychological biases is doubtless valuable for highlighting the potential influences on individual and group perceptions of risk, but it does not tell the whole story. People who need to make actual decisions in the world of business or elsewhere need practical guidance based in reality.

Our work on understanding and managing risk attitude takes a clear practitioner perspective, rather than being academic or theoretical, though the foundation is rigorous and secure. We have laid out elsewhere our insights into the field of risk attitudes in general, and encouraged individuals to enhance their level of emotional literacy as a means of making attitudinal changes where required. Now it is time to focus on groups.

Defining groups

A group may be defined as a number of individuals with a shared purpose. Several characteristics within this definition may vary considerably. For example, a group may be formed from a small number of individuals (with a minimum of two) or a large number (perhaps thousands). The purpose may be short-lived (for example, to make a single decision), the group may have a medium-term existence (such as a project team), or it may be a long-term entity (like a family or a corporation). The group may be gathered together in a single location or geographically dispersed. The degree of commitment of group members to the common purpose may vary. Indeed group members may have different reasons for belonging to the group in addition to the shared common purpose (including hidden agendas), some of which may be contradictory or incompatible with the overall group purpose. The one constant in any group is the fact that it comprises a number of individuals. Consequently, the starting point for understanding group behaviour is to understand the individuals who form the group.

The same is true for risk attitudes: group risk attitude is a function of the risk attitudes held by the individuals within the group. The situation in a group is however considerably more complex, as attitudes, behaviour and culture are not merely additive. The whole is different from the sum of the parts (and not necessarily greater!). In order to understand group risk attitude, it is helpful to explore the various influences which might operate within and upon the group.

Potential influences on group risk attitudes

It is clear that there are a range of influences on the behaviour of individuals who make up groups, including conscious factors, subconscious heuristics and cognitive biases, and affective emotional reactions – the 'triple strand' described in Chapter 1. Part of the operation of the three triple strand elements in group situations is their influence on the collective risk attitude in a particular situation, which in turn drives a group's performance in making decisions. There is also a feedback loop, as illustrated in Figure 4.1, because the experience of the decision-making process and its outcomes (either favourable, neutral or unfavourable) colours the future risk attitudes of the group and its participating individuals.

While we have a reasonably good understanding of how individual risk attitudes are formed and how they can be managed proactively, the situation with groups is less clear. There are multiple influences on how groups operate in general, forming a complex web of factors. When the group context involves uncertainty then the position inevitably becomes harder to discern. It would be helpful to conduct a structured analysis of the factors influencing any group, in an attempt to determine the key drivers.

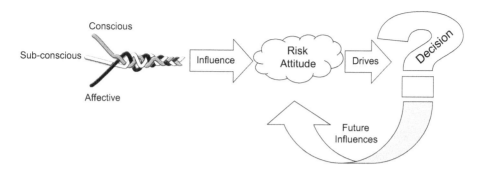

Figure 4.1   Influences on decision-making: 1

INDIVIDUALS WITHIN THE GROUP

Analysis of the factors influencing any group must start with the individuals within the group, since they are clearly a major factor in determining group behaviour. It is evident that not all group members are equal, and they can be separated by a variety of characteristics, including age, gender, organizational status, hierarchical authority, level of experience, personal preferences and motivations, and so on. The question is which characteristics (if any) are relevant to the degree of influence exercised by each individual within the group on its risk attitude?

Some of the characteristics would be difficult to analyze separately and might not be expected to be relevant. Examining differences based on age, gender or race might even contravene discrimination law. Personality-based preferences can be examined using established methods, but it would be difficult to gather a representative number of data points about individuals in decision-making groups to draw sensible conclusions.

Given the data-gathering challenge, one approach might be to use proxy measures to summarize the collective effects of a range of individual characteristics on the behaviour of the group and its risk attitude. Two such potential proxy measures are the perceived levels of *power or influence* of individuals in groups, and the degree of *personal propinquity* perceived by each individual. Both power and propinquity are complex factors with a range of contributory influences, but both have the advantage of being measurable to a degree, allowing them to be used as proxy measures for their underlying drivers.

Table 4.1   Sources of power

•   Referent power. This is where an individual is regarded as a role model by others. It derives from who the person is, rather than what they do, and is based on trust and respect.
•   Expert power. This is based on relevant knowledge and expertise demonstrated through technical competence and specialized skill.
•   Reward power. Some individuals can deliver rewards to others, including financial, emotional, professional status etc., which lead people to defer to them.
•   Coercive power. This fear-based source of power recognizes that some people can impose sanctions (formal or informal) on others in the group if they fail to comply (the opposite of reward power).
•   Legitimate power. This derives from a formal position in the group or organization, which gives an individual authority to impose their view on others.

POWER AND PROPINQUITY AS PROXY MEASURES

There are many sources of power that provide the potential for an individual to influence a situation, as summarized in Table 4.1. While detailed analysis could be possible based on power types, a simple classification of individuals as having high power or low power within a group might be useful as a proxy measure for more complex factors, in order to summarize their potential influence on behaviour and outcomes.

Propinquity is defined as 'nearness in relationship' and represents the degree to which a situation, risk or decision is 'near' to an individual or group, or how much it matters to them personally. As a proxy measure, propinquity is less well researched, but it can be classified on a simple high–low scale and used as a proxy measure in the same way as power.

Together, the two variables of power and propinquity offer a potential model for understanding which individuals might exert more influence on group risk attitude than others. This approach is consistent with existing stakeholder mapping/analysis methods such as the Stakeholder Cube (shown in Figure 4.2) and the Stakeholder Circle™ (Figure 4.3). These methods are based on subjective assessments of a number of variables including both power (called 'influence' in other models) and propinquity (also known as 'interest' or 'vested stake'). For example in Figure 4.2, the 'degree of interest' is an indication of personal propinquity of the stakeholder in question, based on the assumption that people tend to be more active and interested in things that matter to them, either because they are for and willing to back the decision, or against and intending to block it.

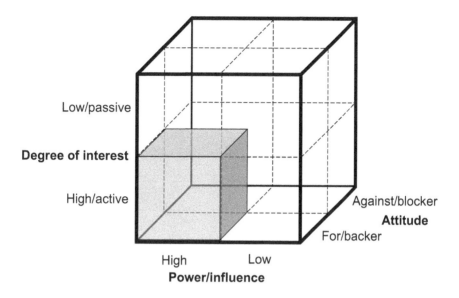

Key: The cube has eight different positions. The highlighted area represents a Powerful Active Backer

Figure 4.2   The Stakeholder Cube

(adapted from Murray-Webster and Simon, 2006)

COLLECTIVE INFLUENCES ON GROUP BEHAVIOUR

Apart from the influence of individuals within the group, there are a number of other collective factors that influence group behaviour and therefore might influence perception of risk and group risk attitude. These include:

- group dynamics

- organizational culture

- national culture

- societal norms.

Group dynamics can be defined as 'the psychological and sociological processes that separate the workings of a group from a random collection of individuals'. It is concerned with the interactions between group members that shape the behaviour of the whole. Group dynamics focuses primarily on small group behaviour and includes the influence of norms, roles, relationships, development, the need to belong, social influence and effects on behaviour. Some aspects of overall group dynamics clearly have strong links with powerful and interested individual stakeholders, for example patterns of dominance and the

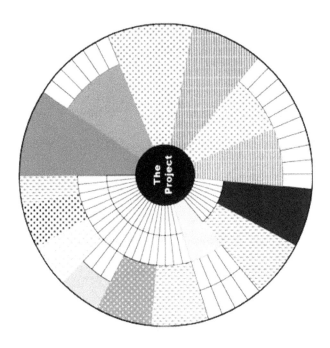

Key: Each segment represents a different stakeholder, with the most important at 12 o'clock, decreasing in importance as you move clockwise. Radial depth represents *power*. Arc width represents *influence (a combination of power and the stakeholder's sense of urgency)*. Closeness to centre represents *proximity to the project (only relevant to stakeholders with lower levels of power)*.

Figure 4.3   The Stakeholder Circle™

(adapted from Bourne, 2007)

style of leadership and followership adopted. However, there are other aspects of group dynamics that are less directly correlated to individuals, for example the maturity or developmental stage of the group, or the group's adopted style for conflict handling.

One specific set of influences on group dynamics are group heuristics (mentioned in Chapter 1) that work as short-cuts to group consensus, but which often result in the group adopting a different perspective or risk attitude from that taken by individual group members. 'Groupthink' is the most well-known group heuristic, although 'risky shift' – the tendency of a group to be more risk-seeking than its constituent individuals – and 'cautious shift' – when the group becomes more risk-averse than its individual members – work in a similar way by creating the illusion of safety in numbers, reducing personal accountability for decisions and skewing the risk attitude adopted by the group. For example a decision-making group might each individually think that diversification into a new market is unlikely to succeed and that the potential rewards do not justify the risky investment, but in a group situation they talk themselves into having a go, with no one individual wanting to appear too cautious in front of their peers.

Organizational culture is defined as 'the basic assumptions and values that operate subconsciously and are "taken for granted" within an organization, and that shape collective beliefs and behaviour'.

Although organizational culture could be viewed as an extension of group dynamics, it has a more permanent and enduring influence. Some organizations have a well-developed culture, built on unifying symbols, common processes and shared behaviour. In such organizations the culture enables cohesion and focus, institutionalizes success and sustains purpose and meaning. Organizational change in such cultures can be difficult. Other organizations, either through design or happenstance, have less unifying cultures. In such organizations it would be easier for particular decision-making groups to do their own thing and adopt decision-making processes and risk attitudes that seem appropriate situationally rather than conforming to 'the way things are done around here'.

National culture covers 'features of the typical values and behaviours of a nation that shape beliefs and expectations'.

The most influential work in this area by researchers including Hofstede (1982), Trompenaars and Hampden-Turner (1998) and Spony (2001) highlights a number of distinct characteristics of national culture that distinguish between nations and influence their behaviour. For example two of Hofstede's diagnostic characteristics (Power Distance and Uncertainty Avoidance) have clear influences on risk attitude and decision-making. According to Hofstede, in some national cultures the norms include a high respect for hierarchical structures (high Power Distance) and/or being uncomfortable when situations are ambiguous and outcomes unknown (high Uncertainty Avoidance). In such cultures there would be a tendency for decisions to come from the most 'powerful' person, and any decision that removed ambiguity would be preferable to a delay that left the situation uncertain. Clearly in some group decision-making situations national cultural differences would have an effect, both on the perception of risk by the decision-making group, and on the dynamics between individuals within the group. Where the decision-making group is made up of individuals from a single (or closely related) national culture, this effect is likely to be absent.

Societal norms represent 'the values and behaviours that are acceptable to the majority of citizens within a particular culture or subculture'. These are often associated with risk-taking behaviour, for example attitudes to smoking in public places, or to driving when under the influence of alcohol or other mood-altering drugs. Although there may be a link between national culture and societal norms in some circumstances, in terms of influence on group risk attitude and decision-making, it is possible to separate the two influences.

A number of influences on group behaviour have been described here. Each is supported by a wide and deep body of research and applied knowledge that can be explored further. It is clear that each influence could matter to a greater or lesser extent depending on the situation, and this is consistent with our overriding position regarding risk attitudes – that they are situational, chosen responses based on perception of the risks present at a particular time.

However, if we want to understand group risk attitudes in order to manage them and their influence on decision-making, it is not enough just to recognize that there are many influences that could affect risk attitude and decision-making. We need to know whether there are any patterns in the degree of influence of each variable, and whether this allows development of strategies to support effective management of group risk attitude.

A working hypothesis

Given the range of factors and influences affecting group decision-making, it would be both interesting and useful to know if any are more influential than others. Being able to prioritize the effect of different factors on groups would lead to improved understanding of the drivers of group behaviour, and may indicate approaches to manage these proactively in order to optimize decision-making performance.

The factors that seem relevant from our experience can be ranked in order of their closeness to the decision, forming a series of influences similar to the ripples in a pool of water (Figure 4.4). *Individuals* would be expected to have the closest relationship with the decision to be made and perhaps those individuals with the most personal interest in the decision might be closer than those who are more disinterested. Outside the individuals making up the *group* lies the group itself, and group dynamics could form the next layer of influence. Beyond the group are the various contexts within which the group exists, including the *organization*, then *society* at large, with the *national and international* settings at the outermost limit. As the distance increases between the various sources of influence and the decision itself, one could expect the strength of influence to decrease (analogous to the physical power–distance law).

The distance of these factors from the epicentre of the decision can be described as *propinquity*. This is defined as 'nearness in relationship' and represents the degree to which something matters to an individual or group. Propinquity appears to decrease through the various influential factors in the following series:

1. Individuals with the power to affect the decision might be expected to have a high degree of propinquity, with lower propinquity for those who are less powerful.

2. The decision-making group itself has an interest in the decision outcome, though the decision might matter less to the group as a whole than it does to the various individuals who comprise the group.

3. The organization to which the group belongs will have an interest in the decision, but the degree to which this matters to the organization is likely to be less than for the group.

4. It is possible that some decisions may have a wider interest for those outside the organization, for example to stakeholders in society at large. However, the degree of closeness in most cases will be much lower than for those in the organization or the decision-making group.

5. A few decisions will matter at national or international levels, especially those made by politicians or executives in global corporations and so on. Propinquity is expected to be lowest at this extreme distance from the point at which the decision is made.

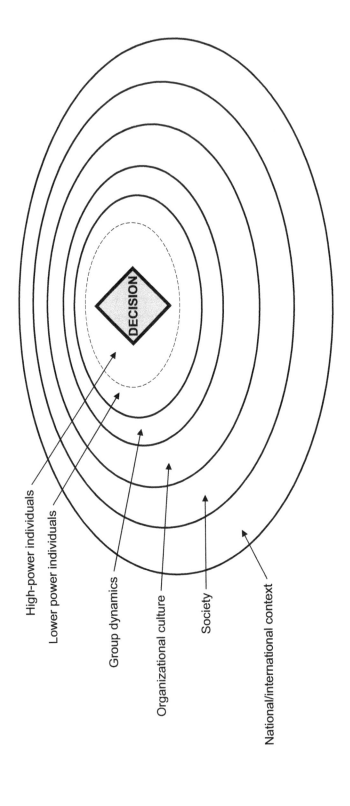

Figure 4.4   Influences on decision-making; 2

This apparent reducing degree of propinquity can be overlaid onto these five factors, as shown in Table 4.2.

Table 4.2   Decreasing propinquity across five factors

Factor	Propinquity
1. Individuals	Very high
2. Group	High
3. Organization	Medium
4. Society	Low
5. National/international	Very low

If the factors influencing a group decision can be ranked by propinquity in this way, then it becomes possible to formulate a working hypothesis relating these to the behaviour of a group when making a decision in an uncertain context. Such a hypothesis could be stated as follows:

The most important influence on any group decision is the individual risk attitude of group members with the highest levels of power followed by the individual risk attitudes of other less powerful group members. Group dynamics and organizational culture exert significant influence, with wider societal and national/international influences having the least impact. This rank order of influencing factors may be driven by propinquity.

Testing the hypothesis

The number of nested variables present in this working hypothesis makes it inappropriate (and perhaps impossible) to design rational, laboratory-based scientific experiments to test it. A process of social enquiry examining influences on decision-making groups in uncertain circumstances is more likely to yield meaningful results. Our approach therefore has been to use a two-phase research programme to analyze retrospective views from members of decision-making groups on the decision processes and decision outcomes for particular decisions.

In the first phase, detailed data have been gathered from a small number of decisions made by groups in a variety of situations. Up to three different perspectives were obtained for these decisions, to explore the varying perspectives of different group members on the same decision-making situation. A total of eight decisions were examined in detail, with responses from eighteen individuals. The questionnaire used to gather data is presented in Appendix B. Details of the decisions are analyzed in Appendix C (sanitized to protect the confidentiality of participating individuals and organizations). These decisions were subjected to a rich interpretative analysis to determine the key drivers influencing the decision-making process and outcome, and the results were used to hone the original hypothesis and design a data-gathering instrument for the second phase.

In the second phase, a web-based survey was used to validate the refined hypothesis, and to gather sufficient data to support a robust analysis. This survey (presented in Appendix D) focused on testing the relative importance of the various factors in influencing the decision-making process and outcome. It also examined the relative strength of the triple strand influences. Survey participants were encouraged to consider only those decisions which they perceived to be both risky and important. Decisions perceived as risky by the respondents were chosen in order to maximize the chance that risk attitudes would have been influential in the decision-making process. Decisions perceived as important were used as propinquity is likely to be more evident and significant in such contexts. A total of 281 responses were obtained from the web-based survey, providing results that are likely to be both meaningful and significant.

The subjective nature of the data-gathering method is fully recognized, since the results represent the perception of those individuals who completed the survey, coloured by multiple biases and other influences. Scientifically rigorous research in this area usually focuses on a single variable in a complex process, and the whole is never tested. This presents researchers with a choice: defensible results based on a constrained and simplified approach; or use of a less rigorous method to generate richer results.

Our motivation here is to unpick the many and varied influences and to understand the relative importance of these from the perception of decision-makers. 'Perception' is the operative word here. In order to improve the management of group risk attitude, decision-making processes and resultant decision outcomes, a deeper understanding is needed of the drivers of group risk attitude *as perceived* by individual members of decision-making groups.

The results of our research are presented and discussed in the next chapter, which provides a rich picture from the detailed decision analysis, supported by a closer examination of the key drivers of decision-making performance.

Exploring Influences on Group Risk Attitude

The two-stage process of social enquiry outlined in Chapter 4 was used to test the hypothesis that the range of factors influencing decision-making groups in risky and important circumstances can be ranked in order of importance, driven by propinquity (that is, the degree to which the outcome matters). Our analysis of the retrospective views and perceptions of members of decision-making groups yielded a number of interesting results. These confirmed some aspects of the original hypothesis and falsified others, leading to a more robust view of the factors that influence the risk attitudes adopted by decision-making groups. This chapter presents the findings from our research.

Research phase 1: rich interpretative analysis

Our first phase of research tapped into the rich source of data available from specific individuals who had been part of a decision-making group. The individuals who responded were drawn from our professional networks. Eighteen responses were received, describing eight decisions (sanitized summaries are in Appendix C). Our analysis sought to uncover the main influences affecting the decision-making process and outcome, and led to a modification of our original hypothesis which was explored during the second phase of the research.

Our original hypothesis in Chapter 4 identified six possible influences on decision process and outcome, and the Phase 1 data-gathering questionnaire (see Appendix B, Section 3) presented these factors to respondents and asked them to rank the factors in order of importance. The hypothesis suggested that the six factors would be ranked in the following order (see Figure 4.4):

> 1st   People with high power
>
> 2nd People with lower power
>
> 3rd Group dynamics

4th   Organization culture

5th   Societal norms

6th   National culture

The hypothesis also suggested that this rank order would be driven by propinquity. If this were true, then closeness to the decision, or the degree to which the decision mattered, would be paramount.

As well as listing the six factors above, the research questionnaire provided respondents with an opportunity to identify additional factors that they perceived to be significant in influencing the decision process or outcome. A significant number of respondents did propose other factors, and nine of these identified some aspect of the decision context as being influential. Examples of influential decision contexts included the fact that the decision was made under time pressure, that the governance for the decision was particularly influential, or that the history leading up to the decision was a key factor in shaping attitudes to the risky situation and behaviours in the decision meeting. This result indicated that our original list of six factors was incomplete, and that 'decision context' should be included explicitly in our subsequent analysis.

Our analysis of the detailed answers indicated that it is also highly likely that those respondents who did not pull out a contextual factor as a separate point might have been including this driver as part of their understanding of organizational culture. For example, some respondents gave comments such as 'the decision was made under time pressure' as an example of organizational culture, where others made the same comment and called it decision context. Consequently we decided to combine 'Other factors: Decision context' with 'Organizational culture' in our analysis of responses in the initial research phase, and to explore these more precisely in the second phase of the research (see below).

RANKING OF INFLUENCES (PHASE 1)

Section 3 of our research questionnaire (Appendix B) listed the six factors and asked respondents first to describe their perception of how influential these had been in the decision that they were describing. Respondents were then asked to rank the six factors (plus any additional factors they had listed) in order of their perception of the strength of influence of each factor on the decision. Where the additional factor was some aspect of decision context, this was combined with organizational culture as described above. The ranked position was then converted directly to a number, with the highest-ranking factor being scored 1, through to the lowest ranked factor scoring 6 (or 7 if an additional factor had been added by the respondent). A mean ranking score was calculated for each factor, with a low score indicating a high perceived ranking. Finally this was converted into a 'Normalized ranking score' between zero and one (with the highest ranking factor set to 1).

Table 5.1 presents the results of this ranking analysis, and compares this with the prediction from the original hypothesis. The normalized ranking score data (in brackets in Table 5.1) are also presented graphically in Figure 5.1.

Figure 5.1 clearly shows that the factors were ranked by respondents in two groups. We describe these as 'primary factors' (ranking first to third) and

Table 5.1   Ranking of influential factors (Phase 1 research)

Factor	Mean ranking score	Rank	Predicted rank
Organizational culture and decision context	2.1 (1.00)	1st	4th
Group dynamics	2.2 (0.95)	2nd	3rd
People with high power	2.4 (0.88)	3rd	1st
People with lower power	4.0 (0.53)	4th	2nd
Societal norms	5.1 (0.41)	5th	5th
National culture	5.3 (0.40)	6th	6th

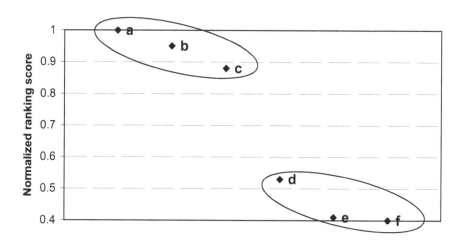

a, organizational culture and decision context; b, group dynamics; c, people with high power; d, people with lower power; e, societal norms; f, national culture.

Figure 5.1   Ranking of influential factors (Phase 1 research).

'secondary factors' (ranking fourth to sixth). The primary factor group includes organization culture and decision context, group dynamics, and high-power individuals. The lower-influence group of secondary factors includes lower-power individuals, wider societal norms and aspects of national culture. The significance of these two groups of factors is discussed further below, in the light of the second phase of the research.

INFLUENCE OF THE TRIPLE STRAND (PHASE 1)

The research questionnaire requested respondents to rate the strength of influence of each of the triple strand elements on the decision process and outcome (see Appendix B, Section 5). To aid understanding, the headline triple strand titles (conscious, subconscious, affective) were replaced in the questionnaire with the following descriptions:

- rational, situational factors, for example familiarity, manageability, proximity or personal propinquity;

- subconscious heuristics, for example stereotyping, groupthink or risky/cautious shift;

- emotions or feelings, for example fear, worry, excitement, revenge, desire to win.

Respondents were asked to select one of 'absent/weak/partial/strong/don't know' for each triple strand group. This was intended to provide initial evidence on the awareness of decision-making groups of these various sets of factors.

Respondents' assessment of the strength of each strand was converted into a mean score, based on absent = 0, weak = 1, partial = 2, strong = 3, don't know = 0. The results are presented in Table 5.2, and suggest reasonable agreement that the conscious strand is a major influence on the decision process and outcome, with over half of the respondents rating the influence of conscious factors as 'strong'. There was less agreement over the importance of the other two strands (indicated by the higher standard deviations), with subconscious factors being rated lowest (a third of respondents said these factors were 'weak' or 'absent').

INITIAL CONCLUSIONS FROM PHASE 1

Two issues are immediately noteworthy from this initial analysis. First is the fact that people with lower power were included by respondents in the group of secondary factors, when our original hypothesis predicted a more prominent influence. Second, comparing the actual ranking with the predicted ranking

Table 5.2   Perceived strength of triple strand influences (Phase 1)

Triple strand group of influences	Mean score	Standard deviation
Conscious	2.6	0.6
Subconscious	1.7	1.0
Affective	2.3	0.9

in Table 5.1 some differences are clear. Ranking was explored in more detail during the second phase of research, and this finding will be discussed further below.

A number of significant conclusions can be drawn from analysis of the first phase of the research, based on the ranking analysis detailed above and supported by a more detailed examination of the specific decision processes as reported by our respondents (see Appendix C).

1. The perceived high importance of contextual factors (such as time pressure to decide) was surprising, but detailed review of the responses indicates that factors of this type provided a focus for the decision-making process and gave meeting participants something to agree on (even if they agreed with little else). Whilst not being the same as organization culture, the effects of decision context appear to be similar. Where decision-makers recognize a common factor either in the organization or in the decision context, it creates a synergy that sustains purpose and meaning for the group. (See Decisions 2, 3, and 4 in Appendix C.)

2. Group dynamics emerged as the second most critical influence from this round of the research. Although some aspects of group dynamics are not directly correlated to individuals (for example the development stage of the group), our respondents specifically linked the influence of group dynamics to the behaviour of people, and in particular to the style of leadership and followership adopted. It is possible that some respondents may have been unable to distinguish the influence of the most powerful person from the influence of the perceived group dynamics led by that person. (See Decisions 1, 2, 5, 6 and 8 in Appendix C.)

3. Group dynamics can make situations more risky than they otherwise would have been. This happens when wider personal factors infiltrate the specific decision context and create conflict.

It is difficult to focus on the issue at hand when the situation is complicated with personal or hidden agendas. For the decisions reported by our respondents, injection of these types of influence into a decision meeting seemed to drive more cautious, risk averse group behaviours, although this may not be true generally. (See Decisions 5 and 7 in Appendix C.)

4. The people perceived as powerful in the decision-making groups tended to get their way, with those who combined high power and high propinquity succeeding most of the time. However, if such individuals were isolated as lone voices in the meeting their influence was reduced, even if they represented a wide constituency of people who were not present. (See Decisions 1, 4 and 5 in Appendix C.)

5. Powerful people make mistakes, and their influence sometimes results in an inappropriate decision being made. One of the reported decisions (Decision 6 in Appendix C) clearly showed how the group were too risk seeking, leaving too much residual risk on the table, to the detriment of the business. Another (Decision 5) clearly showed how the group were too risk averse, taking a precautionary and extremely expensive way forward for the business.

6. When decisions are difficult and there is much disagreement, agreeing to defer a decision feels good and gives the decision-makers a second bite of the cherry at another time. Keeping options open is sometimes an optimal choice, but is often suboptimal, falling foul of the 'lure of choice' heuristic. (See Decision 4 in Appendix C.)

7. The previous history of a decision process leading up to the decision-making meeting is a significant source of bias and cannot be ignored. Such prior experience may influence decision-makers in a variety of ways, including consciously, subconsciously or affectively (that is in any of the ways encapsulated by the triple strand of influences). (See Decisions 5 and 7 in Appendix C.)

8. Only two of the eight reported decisions had potential national cultural implications arising from the involvement of key stakeholders from differing nationalities. This dataset is too small to draw general conclusions, although in both cases respondents reported that national culture was not perceived as being particularly influential in comparison with the other factors. (See Decisions 4 and 8 in Appendix C.)

9.   People with high propinquity seemed to recognize the influence of affective factors (feelings and emotions) more easily. This may be because their strong involvement in the decision process and outcome make them more alert to the feelings of others in the group. The influence of affective factors was also perceived as being lower when the decision was seen as being less important or less risky. This relates to the influence of the triple strand on perception of risk: the more that the uncertainty matters, the more influential are situational factors, cognitive biases and feelings-based drivers. (See Decisions 1, 2, 3, 5, 6 and 7.)

Research phase 2: web-based survey

The second phase of our research used a web-based survey (presented in Appendix D) to further test the original hypothesis, including the refinements indicated by the first phase. We specifically used this phase to obtain a larger dataset which would allow detailed exploration of the relative importance of the various factors in influencing the decision-making process and outcome. Finally the web-based survey was used to examine the perceived relative strength of the triple strand influences. The survey was sent to our networks of contacts who are interested in risk management and organizational change, as well as to members of relevant professional bodies and online discussion groups. A total of 281 responses were obtained from the web-based survey, providing results that are likely to be both meaningful and significant.

The modifications made to reflect learning from the first phase of the research included an expansion of the original list of six factors to eight:

- Inclusion of propinquity (the people to who the decision mattered most) as an explicit factor, separate from power. This was done in order to distinguish the relative importance of these two factors.

- Inclusion of decision context as an explicit factor, separate from organizational culture, because a significant number of respondents in the earlier research had identified this as an influence. This allowed the relative importance of decision context and organizational culture to be explored, and removed the potential for confusion or overlap between the two.

In addition to expanding the set of factors to be considered as influences on the decision-making process and outcome, we also requested survey participants to consider only those decisions that they perceived to be both risky and important. We had originally assumed that individuals participating in the research would automatically consider only decisions of this type when responding. This is important because our research hypothesis relates risk attitude to propinquity. Risk attitudes are more likely to be influential in the decision-making process for decisions perceived to be risky. Similarly propinquity is likely to be more evident and significant in decisions perceived as important. However, one set of respondents to the earlier first-phase research questionnaire had chosen to report on a decision that none of them saw as very important or particularly risky. By directing web-based survey respondents only to consider decisions perceived as both risky and important, we intended to remove this anomaly for the second phase of the research.

Our motivation in conducting this second phase of research was to build on the first phase, and unpick the many influences on decision process and outcome in order to understand their relative importance as perceived by decision-makers.

CONSIDERATION OF RISKS WHEN MAKING DECISIONS

At the beginning of the web-based survey (see Questions 1 and 2 in Appendix D), people were asked whether they had explicitly considered risks before the decision-making meeting, either as individuals or as a group. Nearly all (90 per cent) respondents said that they had considered risks overtly as individuals prior to the decision meeting. Similarly, 55 per cent considered risks as a group before the meeting. These proportions may be artificially higher in our response population because all the web-survey respondents were interested in or aware of risk management and the importance of risk attitudes. Nevertheless it is encouraging that most individuals and the majority of groups expressly consider risk when poised to make important decisions.

We were also interested in whether consideration of risks focused only on uncertainties with negative impacts (threats), or the extent to which upside risks (opportunities) were included, and this was addressed in Question 3. Where risks were considered overtly before the meeting, respondents were divided as follows:

- forty-eight per cent considered only those risks that posed a threat to achievement of objectives;

- five per cent considered only positive risks (opportunities);

- forty-seven per cent said that both threats and opportunities were considered.

This division by consideration of risks is shown in Figure 5.2.

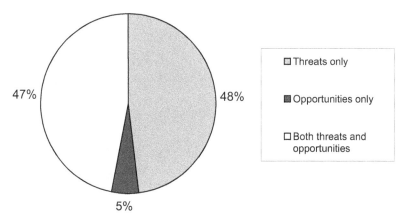

Figure 5.2   Consideration of risks before decision-making

PERCEIVED QUALITY OF THE DECISION

The next question in the web-based survey (Question 4 in Appendix D) asked respondents to assess the extent to which the decision outcome met the organizational objectives, selecting from optimal, reasonable, suboptimal or unacceptable. Only 20 per cent of respondents thought that the decision taken by the group was the right one (that is, optimal), and 64 per cent thought that the decision was reasonable in the circumstances, with the remainder selecting either suboptimal (14 per cent) or unacceptable (2 per cent), as illustrated in Figure 5.3.

Current best practice in risk management recognizes the importance of taking a balanced view of risk that includes threats and opportunities, rather than the traditional threat-only perspective. This is based on the concept that benefits and value can only be maximized if upside risks are proactively identified and pursued. Following this line of thought, we were interested in whether decision quality might be similarly influenced by explicit consideration of opportunities in the risk process. We therefore examined the correlation between consideration of risks before the decision was taken (Figure 5.2) and the perceived quality of the decision (Figure 5.3), separating out those respondents who had only considered threats from those who took the broader view. The data are given in Table 5.3, expressed as percentages of the total number of respondents in each group (noting that there were approximately equal numbers of people in both the 'threats-only' and 'threats plus opportunities' subsets).

These data suggest the possibility that including opportunities in the risk process may result in a higher number of optimal decisions (an increase of

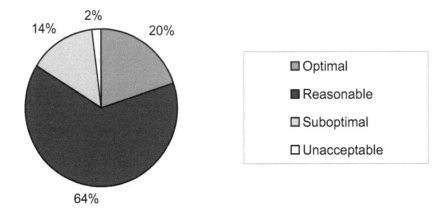

Figure 5.3   Perceived quality of decision outcome

Table 5.3   Correlating consideration of risks with decision quality

Dataset	Perceived data quality			
	Optimal (%)	Reasonable (%)	Suboptimal (%)	Unacceptable (%)
All data	20	64	14	2
Threats only	16	66	16	2
Threats plus opportunities	24	64	10	2

8 per cent over the threat-only result) and fewer suboptimal decisions (down by 6 per cent). However, there are insufficient data to be certain of this conclusion, although it is an intriguing possibility that deserves further investigation.

RANKING OF INFLUENCES (PHASE 2)

Section 3 of the web-based survey addressed the influence of factors on the decision process and outcome. This used the expanded set of factors based on the results of the first phase of our research, adding propinquity and decision context as discussed above. The eight factors listed were presented in random order to avoid biasing responses, and also used descriptive or commonly used terms rather than jargon words (such as 'propinquity'), as follows:

a.   organizational culture

b.   the people in the meeting with high power

    c.   national culture

    d.   group dynamics

    e.   the people in the meeting with less than high power

    f.   societal norms

    g.   the context for the decision

    h.   the people in the meeting who cared most about the outcome.

The survey included two questions to tackle this issue from different perspectives, partly as an internal validation step within the survey, and partly to recognize the different thinking styles adopted by people. The first of these (Question 5 in Appendix D) asked respondents to rate each of the eight factors, describing their perception of the strength of influence on the quality of the decision process and outcome, choosing one of strong, partial, weak, or none. The second question (Question 6) required people to rank the eight factors in order of influence.

Replies to Question 5 were used to calculate a mean 'strength of influence' score for each of the eight factors, based on strong = 3, partial = 2, weak = 1, none = 0. The rankings given in Question 6 were also converted directly to a 'mean ranking score', with a factor scoring 8 if it was ranked first, 7 for second and so on, through to 1 for the factor ranked last. The resulting scores from both questions are given in Table 5.4, which presents the calculated scores as well as normalized rankings (in brackets) derived by setting the highest ranking factor to 1. Finally Table 5.4 also gives a combined ranking for each factor, taking into

Table 5.4   Ranking of influential factors (Phase 2 research)

Factor	Strength of influence score (Q5)	Mean ranking score (Q6)	Combined ranking
People with high power	2.5 (0.96)	6.3 (1.00)	1st =
People with high propinquity	2.6 (1.00)	5.8 (0.92)	1st =
Organizational culture	2.5 (0.96)	5.6 (0.89)	3rd
Decision context	2.4 (0.92)	5.5 (0.87)	4th
Group dynamics	2.3 (0.89)	4.9 (0.78)	5th
People with lower power	1.5 (0.58)	2.8 (0.44)	6th
Societal norms	1.2 (0.46)	2.2 (0.35)	7th
National culture	1.2 (0.46)	2.1 (0.33)	8th

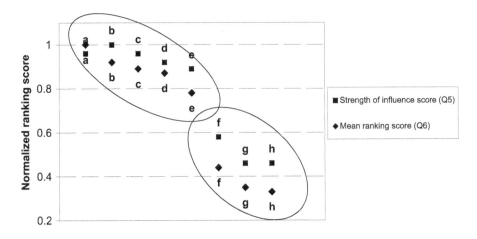

a, people with high power; b, people with high propinquity; c, organizational culture; d, decision context; e, group dynamics; f, people with lower power; g, societal norms; h, national culture.

Figure 5.4   Ranking of influential factors (Phase 2 research)

account the data for both Question 5 and Question 6. The normalized ranking data from Table 5.4 is also shown graphically in Figure 5.4.

The normalized ranking results derived from the two questions are strikingly similar, as shown in Figure 5.4: the only difference is the relative position of high power and high propinquity in the top two positions. This indicates that people responding to the web-based survey were answering consistently when considering the relative perceived importance of the eight factors, irrespective of whether they were assessing the strength of each factor independently (Question 5) or whether they were ranking the factors against each other (Question 6). This consistency is encouraging and supports the validity of the data.

Similarly, it is possible from Figure 5.4 to identify two distinct sets of factors which are perceived to influence decision-making by groups where the decision is seen as both risky and important. There is a clear group of primary factors comprising people with high power, people with high propinquity, organizational culture, decision context and group dynamics. A set of secondary factors can also be distinguished, containing people with lower power, societal norms and national culture. This mirrors the initial conclusions drawn from the Phase 1 results, as is evident when Figure 5.4 is compared with Figure 5.1.

Further support for the existence of two clearly distinct sets of factors comes from a more detailed analysis of how respondents ranked each factor when answering Question 6 in the web-based survey. Figure 5.5 shows how many of the 281 respondents ranked each factor in first, second, third position and so on. Figure 5.5(a) illustrates the primary factor trend with the secondary factor trend shown in Figure 5.5(b). People with high power occupied first position significantly more times than any other factor. People ranking high propinquity, organizational culture and decision context in second, third and fourth positions followed a similar trend to each other. Group dynamics, the lowest scoring of the primary set, was ranked 2–5 in the majority of cases, leading to its inclusion as a primary factor as a result of its high mean score.

DIFFERENCES IN PHASE 1 AND PHASE 2 RANKING

The data obtained through the two-phase research process makes it possible to compare the overall ranking results obtained from the web-based survey used in the Phase 2 research and the more detailed questionnaire returns from Phase 1. This can clearly be seen from the data in Table 5.1 (Phase 1 results) and Table 5.4 (Phase 2 results). The ranking positions are brought together in Table 5.5, which also shows the predicted ranking from our original hypothesis.

It is clear from Table 5.5 that the specific ordering of individual factors within the primary set is different when derived from the Phase 1 data or the Phase 2 results. Both results indicate that the same set of factors are perceived as having the greatest influence on decision-making for risky and important decisions, but the relative strengths of each influence are different. However,

Table 5.5   Summary of factor ranking results

Factor	Phase 2 ranking (from Table 5.4)	Phase 1 ranking (from Table 5.1)	Predicted ranking (original hypothesis)
People with high power	1st =	3rd	1st =
People with high propinquity	1st =	Not included	1st = *
Organizational culture	3rd	1st (combined in Phase 1)	4th
Decision context	4th		Not included
Group dynamics	5th	2nd	3rd
People with lower power	6th	4th	2nd
Societal norms	7th	5th	5th
National culture	8th	6th	6th

* Propinquity is implied by the hypothesis as being the driving force behind all other factors.

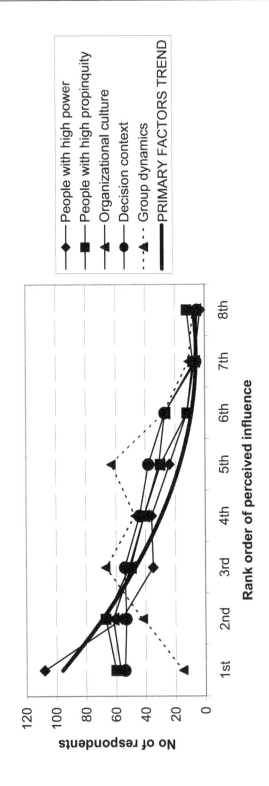

Figure 5.5(a)   Trends for primary factors

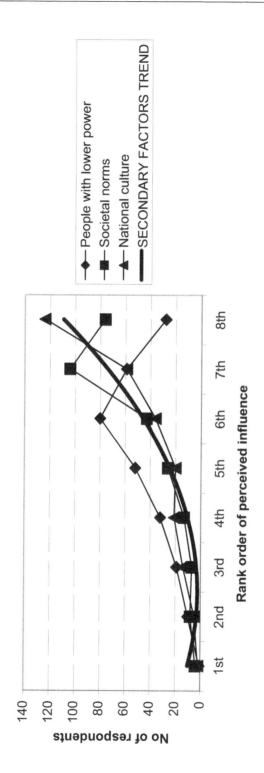

Figure 5.5(b)   Trends for secondary factors

closer examination of the raw data for the primary set of factors indicates that ranking scores are not well separated. For example in Table 5.1 the mean ranking scores calculated from Phase 1 data for the factors in the primary set range between 2.2–2.4. Similarly the Phase 2 strength of influence scores (Table 5.4, Q5 results) for primary factors lies between 2.3–2.6, while the Phase 2 mean ranking scores (Table 5.4, Q6 results) are in the range 4.9–6.3.

The closeness of the various scores for the factors within the primary set suggests that it may not be possible to rank them unambiguously: indeed it may be more useful to treat the primary factors more generically. For example the factors in the primary set can be divided into those which relate to stakeholders (power and propinquity), and those pertaining to the situation (organizational culture and decision context), with group dynamics forming a bridge between the two, as illustrated in Figure 5.6.

This more high-level view of the primary factors influencing groups which make risky and important decisions offers a useful framework for determining how to understand the drivers in such situations, and indicates how they might be managed proactively. This is discussed further in Chapter 6.

INFLUENCE OF THE TRIPLE STRAND (PHASE 2)

A key part of the framework for our understanding of the influences on risk attitude is the triple strand model, dividing influences into conscious, subconscious and affective factors. Phase 1 of our research indicated good awareness of the influence of conscious factors on the decision process and outcome, but less agreement over the importance of the other two strands. A specific question was therefore included in the web-based survey for Phase 2 of the research, in order to validate this finding (see Question 7 in Appendix D). This question asked respondents to rate their perception of the strength of influence of each strand on the decision process and outcome, choosing one of 'strong/partial/weak/absent'.

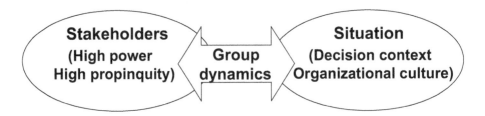

Figure 5.6   Potential relationship between primary factors

The ratings given by respondents for each strand are given in Table 5.6, shown as percentages. These ratings are also converted to a mean score based on absent = 0, weak = 1, partial = 2, strong = 3.

Table 5.6   Percentages of perceived strength of triple strand influences (Phase 2)

Strand	Strong	Partial	Weak	Absent	Mean score
Conscious	66	30	4	0	2.6
Subconscious	21	50	23	6	1.9
Affective	35	41	20	4	2.1

The similarity in mean score between Phases 1 and 2 is striking (comparing Table 5.6 with Table 5.2), validating the original findings on how respondents perceive the strength of the three groups of influences. As before, the majority of respondents are aware of conscious factors and believe they have a strong influence on decision-making. The level of influence of subconscious and affective factors are rated as less strong, though the data are more spread, indicating less agreement between respondents.

In addition to the raw data on triple strand perceptions, the web-based survey allowed us to explore possible links between the perceived strength of influence of each strand and the perceived decision outcome, by correlating responses to Question 7 (triple strand influences) and Question 4 (decision quality). The results of the correlation are shown in Table 5.7 and Figure 5.7. This takes the perception of the quality of decision outcome (one of optimal, reasonable or suboptimal), and indicates the number and percentage of respondents who rated the influence of each triple strand element as either strong or partial. (There were insufficient responses to allow unacceptable decision outcomes to be analyzed in this way, since only seven out of the 281 replies rated decision outcome as unacceptable.)

Table 5.7 and Figure 5.7 show that when decisions were perceived to be optimal, conscious factors were perceived as having a strong or partial influence 100 per cent of the time. In other words, all 55 respondents who felt that the decision-making meeting had produced a good outcome also rated the influence of conscious factors as either strong or partial. By contrast, for optimal decisions, subconscious and affective factors were only perceived as significant influences between 60–65 per cent of the time.

Table 5.7   **Correlating triple strand influence with decision quality**

Perceived quality of decision outcome

<table>
<tr><td rowspan="2">*Triple-strand element perceived as strong or partial*</td><td></td><td>**Optimal**
[total = 55]</td><td>**Reasonable**
[total = 183]</td><td>**Suboptimal**
[total = 35]</td></tr>
<tr><td>**Conscious**</td><td>55
[100%]</td><td>179
[98%]</td><td>29
[83%]</td></tr>
<tr><td>**Subconscious**</td><td>33
[60%]</td><td>135
[74%]</td><td>28
[80%]</td></tr>
<tr><td>**Affective**</td><td>36
[65%]</td><td>146
[80%]</td><td>30
[84%]</td></tr>
</table>

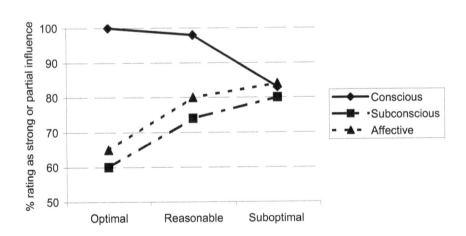

Figure 5.7   **Correlating triple strand influence with decision quality**

For reasonable decision outcomes, conscious factors were seen as only slightly less influential (98 per cent of respondents rated their influence as strong or partial), and subconscious and affective factors appear to be more important (increased to 74 and 80 per cent respectively).

This trend is more apparent for suboptimal decisions, where the influence of conscious factors was perceived to be lowest (rated as significant by 83 per cent of respondents), and that of subconscious and affective factors was seen as highest (with 80–84 per cent of people giving these a high rating).

Viewing the data in Table 5.7 and Figure 5.7 in the other dimension, it appears that decision quality is perceived as being positively correlated with the influence of conscious factors but negatively correlated with subconscious and affective factors. In other words, as the influence of conscious factors is perceived to increase, the quality of the decision outcome gets better (from suboptimal through reasonable to optimal). By contrast, where subconscious and affective factors are seen to have higher influence, the decision quality is lower.

It is not possible to identify the underlying causes of these results from our research data, and this would be an interesting area for further study. The results appear to indicate that the degree of bias exercised by hidden or complex factors is perceived to be lower on good decisions and higher on less optimal decisions. It also appears that people tend to judge that decisions made when emotions are visibly high might be less than optimal; this perception may or may not be valid. Finally the results suggest that subconscious heuristics or cognitive bias such as groupthink, risky/cautious shift or stereotyping are seen to be more significant in decisions of lesser quality; this makes sense as subconscious influences often bias judgement erroneously. These insights from the research are not robustly supported by our research data, but they suggest fruitful areas for further investigation.

Summary of research findings

The starting point for our research was the following working hypothesis:

> *The most important influence on any group decision is the individual risk attitude of group members with the highest levels of power followed by the individual risk attitudes of other less powerful group members. Group dynamics and organizational culture exert significant influence, with wider societal and national/international influences having the least impact. This rank order of influencing factors may be driven by propinquity.*

This original hypothesis was shown pictorially (Figure 4.4) as ripples in a pond radiating out from the decision point, with the people with the highest levels of power nearest the decision epicentre. Our findings now suggest an alternative view, which is less precise but which may be more useful in practice.

Despite refining the number of possible influences on the group decision-making process and outcome from six to eight, our research data do not support a precise rank ordering of the various influences. Instead we have defined two distinct groups of influences on group decisions, which we have termed primary and secondary factors, as shown above in Figure 5.4.

- The primary factors are those which are perceived by people in decision-making groups as having the greatest influence on the decision process and outcome. This group includes those affecting stakeholders with high power and high propinquity, those arising from the situation (decision context and organization culture), as well as group dynamics (Figure 5.6). The absolute priority of each factor within this set cannot be distinguished, since all are important and must be managed. Our detailed analysis however indicates that group dynamics acts as a bridge between the influences exerted by key stakeholders (people with high power and high propinquity) and the influences exerted by the situation (decision context and organizational culture).

- The secondary set of influencing factors are also perceived as being influential in determining the decision process and outcome, but they are seen as less likely than the primary factors to drive group risk attitude and decision-making. Secondary factors include individuals with lower power, wider societal needs and national cultural differences.

The significance of propinquity within the original hypothesis as a driver of influence is supported, particularly when it is combined with high power. It is, however, important to note that analysis of the decision data reported by our respondents indicates that stakeholders will have a strong influence on the decision and process if the decision is close to them personally, whatever their level of power in the situation. This suggests that of the two stakeholder-related factors in the primary group, propinquity may be more influential than power.

We illustrated our original hypothesis using static ripples in a pond (Figure 4.4), but our data supports a more dynamic model. A closer description of what happens in reality is one involving movement, since each of the most significant factors exercises an influence over the others. Retaining the water theme as an illustration, the situation in a decision-making group which has to address a risky and important decision is for the most powerful influence to lead the way in driving the direction of the decision process and outcome. This creates a bow wave effect, with the rest of the influences following on behind, adapting to the dominant force and adding their own influence.

The key findings of the research as represented in Figure 5.6 above indicate two key sources of influence over risky and important decisions made by groups. One set of influences involves stakeholders, particularly those with high power and high propinquity. The second set relates to the situation, arising from the organizational culture and the decision context. The two sets are connected through the influence of group dynamics. Our model suggests that neither stakeholder influences nor situational influences is always stronger than the other, but one or other is likely to lead the way in practice. This results in two main patterns of behaviour exhibited by decision-making groups, as shown pictorially in Figure 5.8:

1.   Where there is a clear leader of the group who has high power and high propinquity (stakeholder factors), the influences of decision context and organizational culture (situational factors) will be perceived as supporting the direction set by the group leader. Group dynamics will also adapt to follow the leader.

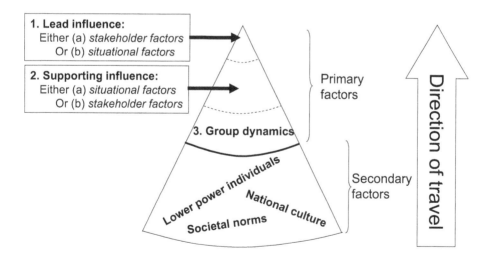

Figure 5.8   Dynamic influences on group decision-making

2.   Alternatively, where there are strong organization norms and a clear decision context (situational factors), these will set the direction for the decision-making process and outcome, and people will adapt their behaviour to fit, even where they have high power and propinquity (stakeholder influences). In this case group dynamics will adapt to follow the culture.

In both of these cases, the primary factors will determine the decision process and outcome, and will be supported by the secondary set of factors, unless other group members are willing to take personal risk to challenge the status quo.

In other words, if there is a strong group leader who is comfortable with the perception of the riskiness of the decision situation (case 1 above), or if the perceived degree of riskiness is consistent with the dominant organizational culture and the context for the decision (case 2 above), then, left unmodified, the risk attitude adopted by the group will follow that of the dominant influence. If the risk attitude of the leader is risk seeking or the organizational culture encourages risks to be taken, then the group is likely to become more risk seeking, unless someone intervenes. This will result in a tendency for the group to accentuate opportunities and discount threats, which may be appropriate in the situation or not. Conversely if the leader is risk averse or the organizational culture discourages risk-taking, then the group will tend to be more cautious unless it is challenged. Such an attitude leading to a focus on threats and dismissal of opportunities may or may not be the right course to take.

Link to managing risk attitudes

The findings from the two rounds of research indicate that risk attitudes are adopted by groups primarily driven by the need to achieve objectives that are of value to the organization (whatever they may be), and in a way that is as harmonious as possible.

This fits with mainstream psychological theories such as Gestalt which identifies a primary human motivation to 'make the picture match', to find patterns and meaning, and to make sense of situations so that a coherent whole is established. Such sense-making motivations are important in sustaining sanity for individuals; no-one can cope when they are surrounded with unfinished business all the time. However, the desire to resolve inconsistencies and produce harmony wherever possible may also be counterproductive when people belong to groups tasked with making risky and important decisions.

In such circumstances, it is unlikely that optimal decisions will be made if the group merely follow the leader or act consistently with the prevailing cultural or contextual norms.

These research findings are interesting in themselves for what they reveal about human motivations and behaviour in group situations which are perceived to be risky and important. However, they also have implications for the practical management of group risk attitude.

The first conclusion is that our existing view of how to understand and manage risk attitude is confirmed and validated. This was summarized in Chapter 3 in our framework of the 'Four A's':

1. *Awareness* of self and others

2. *Appreciation* of self and others

3. *Assertion* of needs and issues

4. *Action* to achieve goals and intentions.

Our earlier work in this area has concentrated on individuals, but it is clear from the research described here that the need to manage awareness and appreciation of self and others is even more fundamental in group situations than it is in personal decision-making. However, this awareness and appreciation cannot be limited to stakeholder-related influences, but must also be extended to include an understanding of situational factors, namely the decision context (including relevant history pertaining to the decision) as well as awareness and appreciation of organizational norms and values. In addition to the need for awareness and appreciation, the results from our research have shown the importance of asserting clear objectives when making group decisions, and of following through in terms of action to achieve those objectives through the decision process.

The Four A's are clearly applicable to groups that make decisions which are perceived to be both risky and important. Beyond the Four A's, however, our research has indicated the need for an important refinement. In some decision-making situations the decision might be perceived as being sufficiently important and risky for people within the group to challenge the prevailing attitudes and behaviours. Instead of simply going with the flow and allowing either a strong leader with high power and propinquity to set the pace, or simply applying accepted organizational norms within this specific decision context, members of a decision-making group may choose to intervene. However, they are only likely to do so if the associated effort and level of personal risk is perceived as worth it. This implies a gap between the first two A's and the last two. Having become aware of the influences on the decision and appreciated their importance, individuals in the decision-making group will only intervene through assertion and action if they think it really matters. Chapter 6 explores the case for adding to the Four A's model in order to bridge this gap.

Implications for Managing Group Risk Attitude

CHAPTER

6

The research described in Chapter 5 aimed to ascertain the most influential factors on the formation of group risk attitude, and the impact of those attitudes on risky and important decisions. A number of insights have emerged, two of which are particularly significant. First is the discovery that there is a distinct set of five primary factors which affect the quality of decision process and outcome. The relationship between these five factors can be described as illustrated in Figure 6.1 (based on Figure 5.6), which shows separately those factors affecting people and those arising from the situation, linked by the operation and influence of group dynamics.

A second key insight is the conclusion that the strongest influence on risky and important decisions made by groups is exercised by either one of the two main types of primary factors, as depicted in the left and right sides of Figure 6.1. Such decisions are most strongly influenced either by the leader – the stakeholder(s) with the combination of the highest power and propinquity– or by the culture – the situational aspects of the decision context underpinned by the prevailing organizational culture. As shown in Figure 5.8, this 'lead influence' of stakeholder factors or situational factors creates a moving force behind which other influential factors follow. Sometimes the effect of the lead influence results in a high-quality decision, but this is not always the case. Groups of people do sometimes make poor-quality decisions, and these can lead to business and personal harm or disadvantage.

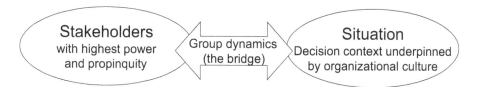

Figure 6.1   Primary factors influencing group risk attitude

This chapter brings together what is already known about managing risk attitudes (as summarized in Chapter 3) with the new insights from our research (from Chapter 5) to produce an innovative and robust approach to managing group risk attitude. Chapter 7 then turns this approach into a set of practical steps that people can use to manage group risk attitude proactively, leading to improved quality of decision-making processes and outcomes.

An initial framework: the Four A's

Our approach to managing risk attitude is grounded in the management theories that we collectively label *emotional literacy*. We have identified three foundational principles that shape this understanding: the Triune Brain concept of brain structure and function, Transactional Analytical life positions ('I'm OK, You're OK') and the Mindset of Choice which enables people to respond rather than react. These combine to suggest that life is largely what we make it; we could be more in control of our destiny than we often realize or accept. When these insights are combined with the traditional understanding of emotional intelligence, the output is a four-step approach to managing risk attitude through applied emotional literacy. We have summarized this as the 'Four A's' model, namely:

1. *Awareness* of self and others

2. *Appreciation* of self and others

3. *Assertion* of needs and issues

4. *Action* to achieve goals and intentions.

The Four A's approach is described in detail in Chapter 3, and we have detailed the link between emotional literacy and managed risk attitude elsewhere (Hillson and Murray-Webster 2007). This general approach to managing risk attitude now needs to be applied to the risk attitude of groups making risky and important decisions. In particular it is necessary to see how this approach addresses the influence on group risk attitudes exerted by the lead influence of either stakeholders or the situation.

The starting point: awareness and appreciation

The Four A's framework starts with *awareness* and *appreciation*, since these are both essential in any situation that is risky and important, either for individuals working alone, individuals who are part of a group, or for the group itself.

Without *awareness*, there is no insight or understanding of the behaviours displayed by ourselves or others. This failure to understand inevitably leads to skewed perceptions and judgements. Lacking awareness leads to a high chance that the situation will manage individuals and the group, rather than them managing it proactively. This is an immature position, and can be potentially dangerous.

If awareness is present but without *appreciation*, then diversity is squashed, prejudices are reinforced, talent is unappreciated and biases become entrenched. Any or all of these impacts will bias perceptions and judgements, leading to poor quality decisions.

This is linked to the earlier discussion (Chapter 2) of the conscious competence learning matrix model, which has four positions arising from the presence or absence of both consciousness (or awareness) and competence (or ability). These are summarized as:

1. unconscious incompetence – we don't know what we don't know;

2. conscious incompetence – we are aware of our shortcomings;

3. conscious competence – we can perform as long as we focus and concentrate;

4. unconscious competence – performance comes naturally.

In our review of this model, we concluded that people can be in any of these four states in regard to their ability to manage their risk attitude, either as individuals or groups. Although the fourth position of unconscious competence might seem an ideal position, we recognized that a fifth position was required in order to manage risk attitude consistently and effectively. Sometimes the natural response is inappropriate when making risky and important decisions. If we just go with the flow and act intuitively with assumed unconscious competence we might make significantly poor decisions. In these circumstances it is better for people to adopt a position of chosen conscious competence and intervene in their thinking processes, if they are to prevent automatic, free-flowing, habitual behaviour when faced with decisions that are risky and important. For the majority of decisions we make throughout each day, habitual unconscious competence is indeed preferable, since it usually offers a safe short-cut to a reasonable outcome. However, for those key decisions that really matter, a more conscious approach is required: one which demonstrates both awareness and appreciation of self and others.

Awareness and appreciation help individuals and groups move from immature and unmanaged management of risk attitude to a more mature approach. In particular, awareness and appreciation of the three distinct elements of the primary factors identified by our research as key influences on risky and important group decision-making (Figure 6.1) is critical, namely:

1. the risk attitude of self and others, particularly those stakeholders who are powerful and are close to the impact of the decision;

2. the decision context and organizational norms that may bias the decision-making group, consciously or unconsciously;

3. the group dynamics and how they may help or hinder an effective decision-making process.

Our research also suggests that awareness and appreciation of the secondary factors (that is less powerful stakeholders, national culture and societal norms) may be important, but it appears that in most cases these factors play a secondary role in determining a good decision process and outcome.

The end point: assertion and action

Awareness and appreciation do not in themselves allow individuals or groups to manage a situation effectively, although they are prerequisites. Management of group risk attitude often requires someone in the decision-making group to make a conscious choice to challenge the prevalent mode of thinking and the natural course of the decision-making process in a way that builds confidence in the final decision, rather than destroying it. To achieve this type of challenge effectively, the last two A's in the Four A's model, *assertion* and *action*, are required.

Such challenging interventions are easier to describe than to carry out. They require highly polished leadership skills to discover and use human discontent or conflict for a constructive, positive purpose. They are also difficult because they need to break into the natural risk attitude adopted by the group as a result of the influence of the leading influence (either stakeholders with high power and propinquity, or the context and norms of the situation).

It may not be so hard for the acknowledged leader of a decision-making group to intervene in the natural flow in order to change direction. However, for others in the group, making such an intervention may carry personal risk as the status quo is unsettled. Our research has demonstrated that in practice individuals tend first to decide whether to align with the risk attitude and behaviour of the leader, or with the norms of the situation. Having made this choice, they can then find it very difficult to influence group processes. This is consistent with the Gestalt view of organizational behaviour, emphasizing that alignment and sense-making are natural human processes. To change group thinking it is necessary to find common ground around which group members can align. If this is to lead to a more successful decision process and outcome, the common ground must not be skewed by perceptual biases. An essential skill in achieving this is the ability to frame context, objectives and questions in a non-biased, inclusive way. Framing the whole on behalf of the group requires an individual to exercise emotional literacy, particularly intentionality (alternatively called impulse control or delayed gratification), emotional control and restraint. It requires a motivation to clarify and open up rather than to justify and close down.

In addition to the ability to frame and present situations so that they can be discussed and debated with minimal bias, managing group risk attitude also essentially relies on leaders having the ability to use discontent for a constructive purpose. The importance of 'constructive discontent' was recognized by US industrialist William Wrigley Junior, who said, 'When two men agree in business, one is unnecessary.' Wrigley knew that constructive discontent is a prerequisite to effective decision-making in groups, in order to harness the power of attitudes that may be ineffective if left unexplored, and to turn these into positives.

Group dynamics can easily become destructive. If this is to be prevented, interventions are required that are assertive, rather than passive or aggressive. It is important to adopt an approach to conflict resolution that is creative, using optimism and appropriate humour to 'oil the wheels', and exercising uplifting human behaviours and an attitude of abundance.

All of this leads us to two conclusions:

1.   It is not always necessary to move from the first two A's of *awareness* and *appreciation* to the last two A's of *assertion* and *action*. This is only required if there is a significant risk that the dominant risk attitude of the lead influence (that is, the leader or culture, whichever is prevailing) will lead the group towards a poor-quality decision. If awareness and appreciation lead to the conclusion that the unmanaged group risk attitude is appropriate, no further action is needed.

2.   Where there is a significant risk of a poor decision-making process
      or outcome arising from the unmanaged risk attitude of the
      group, then intervention is required. This is likely to be difficult
      for individual members of the decision-making group, especially
      if they hold strong views and perceptions of the situation and the
      'right' outcome. In this case a neutral facilitator can play a vital role,
      relieving the participating group members of the need to manage
      the group's risk attitude, and allowing them to concentrate on the
      decision itself.

As a result, we have concluded that although the Four A's model provides
a sound foundation, it is insufficient to describe all the elements necessary for
successful management of risk attitude for groups who are making risky and
important decisions. The first two A's, *awareness* and *appreciation*, are always
required. However, the last two, *assertion* and *action*, may not be needed in
every situation. There is a gap between the first two A's and the last two,
requiring an additional step to determine whether to move from awareness
and appreciation through to assertion and action. There is also a need to define
what is to be done when assertion and action are deemed to be inappropriate.
Consequently the Four A's model needs to be refined and expanded.

Bridging the gap: additional A's

The Four A's model clearly presents a logical sequence of steps in order to
understand and manage risk attitude. However, something else is needed
between awareness and appreciation (the first two A's) and assertion and
action (the second two A's). To understand what is required here, we can find a
parallel in the traditional risk management process, for example the one shown
in Figure 6.2. The first major step in any risk process (after the initiation step) is
identification of the risks. However, not all risks are treated with the same level
of attention and energy. Risk identification is not immediately followed by risk
response planning. Between these two is the risk assessment step, where the
significance and importance of each identified risk is determined. Risks with
low probability, impact or urgency may be treated as low priority, and perhaps
may not even be addressed proactively at all. Other risks which are assessed
as having high probability, major impact on objectives and high urgency will
receive greater attention.

In the same way, it is not necessary to attempt to manage group risk attitude
proactively in every decision situation. Of course, there will be some situations
where unmanaged group risk attitude will significantly affect objectives, either

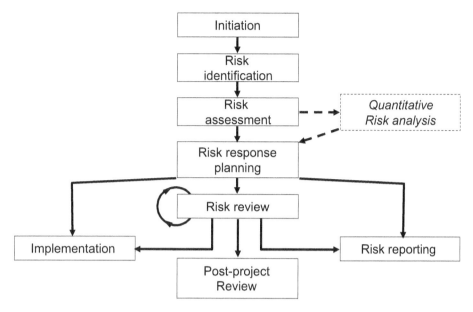

Figure 6.2   A typical risk management process

(adapted from Hillson and Simon, 2007)

for good or for ill, and awareness and appreciation allow these situations to be identified. This is analogous to risk identification in the risk process. Where awareness and appreciation indicate that there is a risk to the decision quality which really matters, then assertion and action will be necessary, which corresponds to the risk-response planning step in the risk process. Conversely, if the conclusion from awareness and appreciation is that the prevailing risk attitude is unlikely to prejudice the decision-making process and outcome, then no assertion or action is required.

Just as in the risk process, risk assessment sits between risk identification and risk-response planning, so there needs to be a fifth *assessment* step inserted into the Four A's model to decide whether it is worth going from awareness and appreciation through to assertion and action.

There is another important lesson to draw from the standard risk management process, which can be used to refine the Four A's model. Not all risks need to be actively managed. Risk management offers a range of proactive response strategies (avoiding, transferring or reducing threats; exploiting, sharing or enhancing opportunities). Where a proactive response is not appropriate, affordable or actionable, residual risks need to be accepted. However, adopting an acceptance strategy for a risk is not the same as ignoring it.

Accepted risks have a nominated risk owner who is responsible for monitoring the situation and implementing a contingency or fallback plan if predefined trigger conditions occur. The risk owner may also reassess the risk and decide that it is no longer appropriate to accept it, in which case an alternative more proactive response strategy is put into place.

The same principles apply to managing group risk attitude when assessment indicates that it is not necessary to intervene. In this case, the steps required are first, awareness and appreciation, in order to understand the decision-making situation and context, followed by assessment to determine whether intervention is required. If assessment indicates that the unmanaged group risk attitude poses no threat to the decision-making process or outcome, then the prevailing risk attitude can be *accepted*. This forms a sixth A to be included in the model.

It is also important to recognize that accepting the existing group risk attitude does not mean it will never be challenged. In the risk process, accepted risks are actively monitored, and contingency or fallback plans may be implemented if necessary. They are also reassessed and different response strategies may be selected if the risk becomes unacceptable. In the same way, some group risk attitudes may be accepted in the short term but may need to be managed more actively at some later point. A particular group risk attitude may be accepted over a short period of time (for example within the bounds of a single decision-meeting where a stakeholder has decided in advance not to intervene unless a particular situation arises). However, the same group risk attitude may be challenged later or in the longer term (for example if the same group is making a series of risky and important decisions), with use of assertion and action as appropriate.

This discussion, taken together with our research results, leads us to a new model for managing group risk attitude, which we can call the 'Six A's', as shown in Figure 6.3. This starts with awareness and appreciation, looking at the key influences on the decision-making process and outcome (particularly the primary factors, though secondary factors such as national cultural differences should not be ignored). Next comes assessment, to determine whether the unmanaged group risk attitude is likely to lead to an acceptable outcome or not. Where the assessment step indicates that intervention is required to modify the prevailing risk attitude of the group, assertion and action are needed to make the necessary change. If on the other hand assessment shows that the existing group risk attitude is unlikely to have a detrimental effect, the current risk attitude can be accepted (although it must be monitored and reassessed periodically, which may lead to assertion and action at a later time).

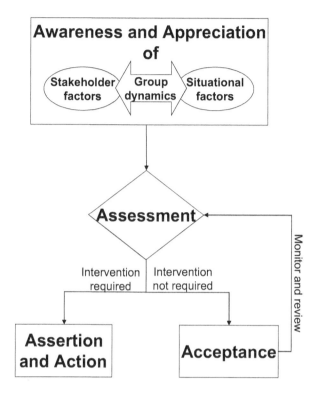

Figure 6.3   The Six A's model

Barriers to managing group risk attitude

Figure 6.3 brings together all of our research into the management of risk attitude into one model, the Six A's. However, the simplicity of this model should not lead us to think that the process is simple to manage. There are a number of barriers that need to be overcome if group risk attitude is to be managed effectively. These include:

1.   inappropriate alignment

2.   wrongly perceived assertion

3.   the lone voice

4.   contributing vs facilitating

5.   unsuccessful interventions

6.   cross-cultural implications

7.   corporate habits.

Each of these barriers is discussed below, illustrated with an example from the decisions analyzed during our research or from our wider experience. Overcoming these barriers has implications for the effective management of group risk attitude, and the next chapter describes a range of practical steps to move forward.

ALIGNING IS NATURAL, BUT ALIGNING WITH THE WRONG THING IS INEFFECTIVE

Organizational behaviour theories such as Gestalt emphasize the natural human tendency to seek alignment in order to reduce conflict and maximize sense-making. Sometimes, however, groups align around the wrong thing, and it becomes necessary to break into this in order to reach a more effective solution. The following factors are important in supporting such realignment:

- framing and the use of language to present alternatives in a non-biased and non-threatening way;

- understanding and using the power bases in the meeting effectively;

- intentionality, delaying gratification in exchange for a better longer-term outcome;

- emotional honesty and restraint, managing your own anger, fear, delight, enthusiasm appropriately;

- an ability to be assertive and use constructive discontent to channel energies into a positive outcome.

In one of the detailed decisions analyzed (see Decision 6 in Appendix C), the group were almost completely aligned on the decision outcome. The decision was supported by the most senior person (the Chief Executive), and also by the programme manager who had led the work and most other people in the decision-making meeting. A few were more sceptical and cautioned restraint, but their power base was not strong enough to redirect or halt the momentum on the direction of the ensuing decision. The decision was made to launch a new product on time, even though it had not been completed to specification. The result was a financial disaster for the company. This indicates that alignment in itself is not sufficient to ensure a good decision outcome.

THERE'S A FINE LINE BETWEEN ASSERTION AND (PERCEIVED) AGGRESSION OR MANIPULATION

An intervention which is intended to be assertive can easily be perceived as aggressive or manipulative, if the appreciation step has not been completed effectively. Assertive interventions are coloured by a whole range of aspects of communication, including tone of voice, the words used, non-verbal gestures and facial expressions. If humour is used this can easily be misinterpreted if there is not a common platform of awareness and appreciation on which to build. From foundations of awareness and appreciation, a creative conflict resolution approach, focused on win/win and built upon a belief of 'I'm OK, You're OK' can be adopted.

One of the detailed decisions analyzed (Appendix C, Decision 7) showed this clearly. In this case honourable assertive intentions were interpreted as manipulation, because some group members were not aware of themselves or others, and/or did not appreciate the perspectives of others. This was a clear case of conflict arising when a decision needed to be made, when the situation may have been avoided through more open and honest communication earlier in the decision-making process.

Although assertion is good and sometimes necessary, without awareness and appreciation it can be misunderstood by others in the decision-making group. It is also possible for the assertive person to go 'over the edge' into aggression or manipulation if they do not maintain a sufficient degree of self-awareness.

IT'S HARD TO BE A LONE VOICE

If an individual is in the position of holding a view which is contrary to the rest of the decision-making group, it is very difficult to break into the consensus, even if the person has great influencing skills and a persuasive argument.

This situation occurred in one of the decisions reported by our respondents, where one powerful stakeholder who cared a lot about the decision outcome wanted a different outcome from the rest of the powerful stakeholders (see Decision 1 in Appendix C). Interestingly, this person was representing a large number of others not present at the meeting. In this particular example, the decision outcome has turned out to be successful, although this was only predicted rather than known at the time the decision was made. For the person with a differing perspective to have had more of an influence at the meeting, they needed to find ways of being heard among the majority view, perhaps by lobbying or other influencing prior to the meeting. Sometimes such lobbying is unsuccessful, in which case it may be best for the lone voice to make their contribution clearly during the decision meeting, then allow the process to take its course.

BOTH CONTRIBUTING TO AND MANAGING THE DECISION PROCESS CAN BE TOO DIFFICULT

If a decision is risky and important, a neutral facilitator can be very useful to frame the situation, uncover and challenge positions and perceptions, allow creative alternative positions to be explored, and help the process along with suitable optimism, humour and activities to unfreeze entrenched positions.

This was a significant influence on one of the decisions analyzed (Decision 3), where the process to make an important and very risky decision for the business was managed by an internal neutral facilitator. This person organized the process, brought the players together in advance to gain a deeper awareness and appreciation of each other's views, and ensured that the conflicting stakeholder positions were reconciled and a way forward was agreed that was optimal for the business.

The role of a neutral facilitator is valuable in many ways, including the fact that it releases key stakeholders to play a full part in contributing to the decision-making process.

TAKING A CHANCE DOESN'T ALWAYS PAY OFF

As with all risks, individuals and groups in decision-making situations 'win some and lose some'. Despite our best endeavours, there are some situations that just don't return the expected result. This is particularly true when individuals in decision-making groups decide to intervene against the prevailing group risk attitude. Such interventions involve personal risk, and inevitably some decisions to intervene and attempt to manage group risk attitude will be unsuccessful. Dealing with this requires resilience and relative regard, which are key elements of applied emotional literacy.

Resilience allows a person to bounce back and be able to manage any stressful side-effects of having taken a personal risk but being unsuccessful. Relative regard is important to maintain confidence in oneself whilst at the same time appreciating the positions of the other parties. It would be perfectly natural in such a situation to resort to blaming yourself, or blaming others for the situation, but this is an immature position to take.

In one of the decisions analyzed (Decision 5), the group risk attitude was influenced almost entirely by the position of the most senior person who was unyielding to attempts to consider alternative solutions. One stakeholder decided to intervene and assert another position using all the leadership and influencing skills they could muster. They failed to influence the position of the most senior person, and therefore the group followed the most senior person into a decision that was more costly for the organization than it needed to be. This decision eroded value for the organization, although it met the needs of the senior person and most of the decision-making group.

CROSS-CULTURAL GROUPS HAVE ADDED COMPLICATIONS

Although the influence of national cultural differences were relatively less important than other factors in our research, despite a number of the decisions analyzed involving people from multiple national backgrounds (Decisions 3, 5 and 8 in Appendix C), these influences cannot be ignored. It is particularly important to appreciate the influence of national cultural norms on the expectations of individuals. For example, a person from a culture where hierarchy is highly respected and there is large power distance between bosses and subordinates (for example France or India) is much more likely to follow the leader than a person from a culture which values each individual's contribution equally (for example the Netherlands or Sweden). Our research does not allow us to comment in detail on the role of national cultural differences, apart from acknowledging the importance of being aware of and appreciating cultural influences on perception and behaviour as a critical step in understanding and managing group risk attitude.

CORPORATE HABITS CAN BLIND US

Our research clearly indicated the significant influence of organizational culture on group risk attitude and decision-making, and highlighted that where the influence of corporate culture would lead to inappropriate risk-taking, it must be understood and managed.

The natural tendency for individuals to align with organizational norms is a double-edged sword. Organizational cultural sameness is highly desirable in order to sustain purpose, meaning and cohesion. It becomes dangerous when it leads to automatic habitual decision-making processes that are never challenged.

Our research did not examine explicitly the effect of systematic organizational biases that skew decisions. However, our wider experience indicates that these exist and it is important to understand them if we are to appreciate group behaviour in risky and important situations. One of our client organizations wants all decisions to be backed up by data rather than to be based on intuition and feelings. As a result they routinely delay decisions until they have 'enough' information (though it is not clear how much is enough). This organization has evidence from the wider market that they are losing strategic advantage by being too cautious and slow when making investment decisions. Another organization is systematically biased by the desire for people to reach challenging 'stretch' targets. The external competition in the marketplace is matched by an internal competition between managers to achieve more and more challenging targets. This culture drives risk seeking behaviour and decision-making that is more macho than meticulous. As a result, managers in this organization are increasingly becoming burned-out and unable to make realistic assessments of what constitutes appropriate risk-taking.

Summary

Our research has led to a new model for understanding and managing group risk attitude, especially in the context of groups making decisions which are perceived to be both risky and important. The Six A's model includes awareness, appreciation, assessment, assertion, action and acceptance, as illustrated in Figure 6.3. Properly applied, the Six A's provide a framework for managing group risk attitude, which parallels the core steps of the standard risk management process: first identify the challenge, then assess whether action is appropriate, followed either by response planning and implementation, or by acceptance and monitoring of residual risks.

Each of the Six A's is important, and the first two are fundamental. Without awareness and appreciation of self and others, decision-making processes in risky and important situations will always be immature, and likely to produce suboptimal outcomes with a significant potential to erode value. With the right level of awareness and appreciation, assessment may indicate that an intervention is necessary, in which case we can use assertion and action to maximize the chance of success. Alternatively where assessment suggests that the influences on group risk attitude are benign and the existing decision-making process is appropriate, we can choose to accept the unmanaged outcome.

This chapter has taken existing knowledge about managing risk attitude as a route to improved decision-making, and consolidated it with our research findings based on real decisions made by groups of people in real organizations. The result is the development of a simple process for understanding and managing group risk attitude, embodied in the Six A's model, together with identification of some barriers to its effective implementation. Chapter 7 translates these findings into practical steps which groups and organizations of all types and sizes can apply.

PART III

Effective Group Decision-making Through Managed Risk Attitude

Practical Steps for Managing Group Risk Attitude

Managing risk and making decisions

Reviewing what is already known about understanding and managing risk attitude (Part I of this book) confirms that this is a fascinating though complex topic. The implications are also widespread, as the adoption of a particular attitude to risk has a major influence on many important aspects of life and business. Two areas which are especially interesting are managing risk, and making decisions.

Risk management is important because it is a pervasive requirement that people must deal with risk. The ability to manage risk effectively is relevant in a broad variety of settings. We are faced with risk in our personal lives (relationships, health, families, careers, pensions, and so on), in the world of business (technology change, reputation issues, contractual commitments, partnerships and supply chains, and so on), and in wider society (demographic trends, environmental change, pension provision, international politics, security and terrorism concerns, and so on). In each of these areas, we are challenged to manage risk effectively, in order to survive and prosper. Our success is measured by our ability to achieve our objectives in the face of the prevailing odds, which may of course be stacked against us or in our favour. The importance of risk to every area of human endeavour is reflected in the most basic proto-definition of risk which we have discussed elsewhere, namely that 'risk is uncertainty that matters'. It is this characteristic of risk, that by definition it matters, which makes risk management an essential competence.

Decision-making is also important, because it is a fundamental human ability. Multiple decisions are made by everyone every day, from the youngest child to the wisest sage. They are required at all levels in human society, including families, communities, organizations, businesses and nations. The ability to make good decisions will determine the quality of life that follows, and separate those individuals and groups who obtain their goals and those who do not (although we discussed earlier the difficulty in defining what makes a 'good' decision). Each decision changes the potential futures available to those who are affected by the outcome, filtering out some options and creating new possibilities.

The two areas of risk management and decision-making also intersect and overlap (as illustrated in Figure 7.1), because the decision process includes the following essential risk-related elements:

- assessment of the risk associated with the decision, including both threats and opportunities;

- determination of the most appropriate response to the level of risk exposure;

- inclusion of risk response actions within the decision implementation plan.

Equally the typical risk management process (set scope and objectives, identify risks, assess their significance, develop and implement responses, review and update, close and identify lessons) requires decisions to be made at many points in the process. Decisions required during the risk process include:

- What is the scope of the risk process?

- What risk threshold reflects the level of risk exposure which is acceptable to key stakeholders?

- How much risk is too much risk?

- What types of risks are important?

- How should risks be prioritized?

- What analytical techniques should be used?

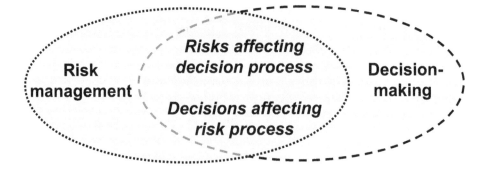

Figure 7.1   Overlaps between risk management and decision-making

- How uncertain is any particular risk, and what might its impact be?

- Which of the various response strategies should be adopted for a given risk?

- How will we know if these strategies are effective?

- Who needs to know about risk exposure, and what do we tell them?

- How can we avoid making the same mistake again, or be sure not to miss a similar opportunity?

The role of risk attitudes

Given the importance of the two areas of risk management and decision-making, and their intimate association with each other, it is essential that we understand anything that might influence effective management of risk or the making of appropriate decisions. Clearly risk attitudes come under this heading. We have defined risk attitude as 'a chosen response to uncertainty that matters, influenced by perception'. We have seen that risk attitude affects the management of risk, through its influence on the risk appetite of key stakeholders, and its ability to lead to inaccurate assessments of risk or inappropriate choice of risk responses and so on. Risk attitude also affects decision-making, particularly through its effect on the risk-related elements of the decision process outlined above. Consequently it is vital that we are able to both understand and manage risk attitude.

There are, however, two complications to achieving this aim. First, everything mentioned above applies to both individuals and groups: the importance of managing risk, the need to make decisions, the linkages between risk and decision-making, and the influence of risk attitude. While the characteristics of these areas are quite well understood in their application to individuals, the situation is less clear in relation to groups. This is because groups are more than the sum of their individuals. The influence of risk attitude on groups in general, and on group decision-making in particular, is a complex web of overlapping factors, deriving from the individuals who are in the group, their interactions with one another, and group-level influences. Our research described in Part II has explored these factors and reached some important conclusions on how they affect the way groups make decisions which are perceived to be both risky and important.

Our use of the word 'perceived' in the last sentence is significant. Perception is the second main complicating factor when attempting to understand and manage risk attitude in relation to group decision-making. Riskiness and importance are in the eye of the beholder(s), and in this area, perception is reality. It is difficult for external observers to diagnose accurately how individuals are truly perceiving a given situation, and it is doubly difficult when working with groups. We know that risk attitude is *personal* (faced with a particular uncertainty, not every individual thinks the same, perceives the same, or adopts the same risk attitude). Risk attitude is also *situational* (a particular individual or group does not adopt the same risk attitude in every setting). Both of these characteristics are greatly influenced by perception.

Perception in turn is subject to a number of underlying influences, which we have described as the triple strand, comprising conscious factors, subconscious factors and affective factors. Through their influence on perception, the three strands are important drivers of risk attitude, for both individuals and groups, affecting the decision-making process and the ultimate decision outcome (Figure 7.2).

New research insights

Our research has revealed some new insights into what drives groups when making decisions which are perceived to be both risky and important.

The results that we have described in Chapter 5 led us to revise our hypothesis, and they support the view that influences on group risk attitude and decision-making fall into primary and secondary sets:

- The primary factors include individuals with high power and high propinquity plus the decision context and organization culture, joined by group dynamics. The absolute priority of each cannot be

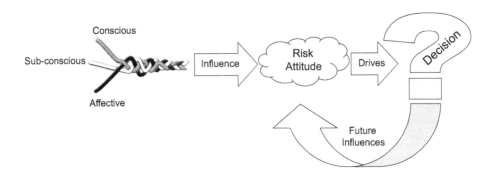

Figure 7.2   The triple strand, risk attitude and decision-making

distinguished: all are important and must be managed. It appears however from the detailed analysis that group dynamics acts as a bridge between the influences exerted by stakeholders (people with high power and high propinquity) and influences exerted by the situation (decision context and organizational culture).

- The secondary set includes individuals with lower power, wider societal needs and national cultural differences. While these remain influencing factors, they are less likely to be primary drivers of group risk attitude and decision-making.

The significance of propinquity within the original hypothesis as a driver of influence is supported, in particular when combined with high power, although those stakeholders, whatever their power, will have an influence if the decision is close to them personally.

We have also produced a new framework within which these areas can be addressed using applied emotional literacy. Based on our research findings, we have expanded our original Four A's framework into the Six A's model (Figure 7.3), and we have made explicit the steps required for active management of risk attitudes in an uncertain group decision-making situation.

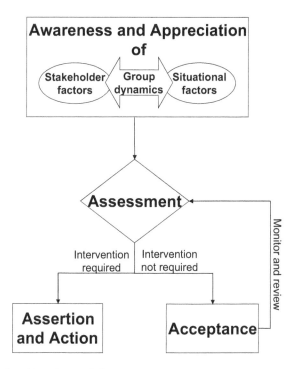

Figure 7.3   The Six A's model

There are a number of barriers that prevent implementation of the Six A's model from being as simple as the diagram suggests. The next section presents a series of specific practical actions which address the barriers for each of the Six A's. Implementing these simple steps will ensure that each of the Six A's is performed effectively and appropriately.

So what? From principle to practice

So far, so good. The theoretical foundation is sound, and the research findings give a clear indication of the way forward. We now need some practical advice on how to implement these principles. The reader who has followed our argument to this point is likely to be saying, 'Yes, I agree, but how do I do it?' The remainder of this chapter lays out our practical recommendations to operationalize and embed the Six A's in the everyday behaviour of decision-making groups. Our list is presented in Table 7.1, and is initially structured in terms of the Six A's, indicating how each step can be accomplished in practice. After describing our recommended actions, alternative ways of structuring the implementation framework are presented.

Table 7.1   Recommended actions, matched to the Six A's

Six A's	Relevant recommended actions
Awareness	A1.1 Develop individuals
	A1.2 Embed organizational learning
	A1.3 Review organizational culture
	A1.4 Perform stakeholder analysis
Appreciation	A2.1 Define clear criteria for decision-making groups
	A2.2 Promote and demonstrate relative regard
Assessment	A3.1 Define meeting parameters
	A3.2 Decide whether to intervene to protect objectives
Assertion	A4.1 Set appropriate meeting culture
	A4.2 Adopt appropriate meeting behaviours
	A4.3 Use a facilitator where appropriate
	A4.4 Challenge inappropriate situations
Action	A5.1 Use power appropriately
	A5.2 Prevent propinquity from biasing judgement
	A5.3 Retain focus on objectives
Acceptance	A6.1 Define triggers for intervention

Awareness

A1.1 Develop individuals. The foundation for a good decision-making group is the individuals who make up the group. Individuals with a high degree of self-awareness will naturally enhance the likelihood of a self-aware decision-making group. Organizations should identify those staff whose roles require frequent decision-making in situations which are perceived to be both risky and important. These individuals should be supported through a personal development programme aiming to increase their personal emotional literacy. Such a programme is likely to be multifaceted, and include elements of education, coaching and mentoring, job rotation and so on. Personal diagnostic tools may be useful to increase levels of self-awareness and indicate areas requiring personal development. Such a tool may be one of the many emotional intelligence diagnostics referenced in Appendix E, or one of the instruments that indicate personal preferences and motivations to work, for example the Myers–Briggs Type Indicator or the Spony Profiling Model (the relevance to risk attitudes of both these tools is discussed in Chapter 2).

A1.2 Embed organizational learning. The organization should develop a structured and consistent approach to learning from experience. This should include regular review of all completed risky and important decisions, identification of lessons to be learned for the future, recording of such lessons in an accessible knowledge base, and routine querying of the knowledge base for appropriate lessons when a new decision-making situation is initiated. Investment in formal knowledge management may be appropriate for some organizations, while others may simply need to proceduralize the lessons-learned process and ensure its effective implementation.

A1.3 Review organizational culture. A cultural audit can be undertaken to analyze prevailing norms across the organization. This should include an exploration of the values, beliefs and behaviours of the organization as embodied by its leadership at various levels, as well as evidence from policies and procedures. The aim is to understand 'the way we do things around here', and determine whether any aspects of organizational culture might be hindering effective decision-making or adoption of appropriate risk attitudes. Where such an audit indicates areas requiring adjustment, the senior management of the organization should initiate a change programme, clearly defining the desired culture, with its associated values, beliefs and behaviours. An organizational culture change programme is not an insignificant undertaking, and must only be done if senior management are serious about following through to fully implement a different way of working. Staff at the working level will easily spot any inconsistencies between declared intentions to change and protected areas of management privilege or resistance.

A1.4 Perform stakeholder analysis. The standard decision-making process should always include a full stakeholder analysis as part of its initiation. A recognized framework should be used, such as the Stakeholder Cube described in Chapter 4. Where there are key stakeholders who are relevant to many decisions situations within an organization (such as a major customer group, an industry regulator, or a trade union), it might be useful to make a standard analysis of these players available to all decision-makers within the organization. All stakeholder analyzes should explicitly address the dimensions of power (influence) and propinquity (interest), because the research reported earlier indicates that these are significant factors in determining a stakeholder's influence over a decision-making situation.

Appreciation

A2.1 Define clear criteria for decision-making groups. The organization should clearly define criteria and thresholds for both riskiness and importance as applied to decision-making situations. Such criteria should be defined in a layered and scaleable way, applicable to the many levels of decision-making that occur within an organization (the strategic, divisional, operational, tactical, and so on). This allows decision-makers to determine unambiguously whether their decision is risky and important. For example a bid decision may be considered to be above the threshold if the price exceeds a given value, or the contract terms are onerous, or the technological solution is innovative and so on. A strategic decision may be deemed risky and important if it affects the organization's brand values or reputation, or if it affects more than three operating units. When criteria are defined at different organizational levels, care must be exercised to ensure that they are coherent and aligned. Riskiness and importance criteria must then be applied as part of the scoping and framing step of the decision-making process, to determine the type of decision being taken. When a decision is determined to be both risky and important, particular care must be taken to understand and manage the influences on risk attitudes of group members during the decision-making process.

A2.2 Promote and demonstrate relative regard. This is a difficult but fundamentally important step to take, and requires highly developed and mature leadership. Promoting and demonstrating relative regard includes valuing differences and diversity, trusting others and using language and meeting behaviours that are inclusive, not exclusive. It requires moderation or control of those natural competitive tendencies or desires which lead us to put others down, value our own ideas above those of others, or exhibit behaviours in groups that close down contributions from others. It requires the value of everyone's contribution to be understood and appreciated in a fair and just manner. Individuals must then take responsibility for sometimes not winning, but being confident that they have had a fair hearing and are appreciated, so their personal power is not diminished by the process. Most importantly, all of these things must actually be demonstrated in practice, not merely stated in the management rhetoric. These actions must particularly be lived by each individual decision-maker in the organization. Practically, progress towards achieving this goal will be supported by:

- human resource policies and procedures that communicate those behaviours that are acceptable, and manage those that are unacceptable;

- support and development for leaders;

- resilience to support continuous improvement, recognizing that human behaviour is complex and rarely changes overnight.

Assessment

A3.1 Define meeting parameters. Every decision-making meeting needs clear parameters defining its scope and purpose. Action A2.1 above outlines the need to define the terms 'risky' and 'important' within the context and objectives of a particular organization. These two factors are key parameters in determining the type of decision-making meeting required. The organization should define a sequence of decision-making situations, with the lowest level decisions (low risk or of minor importance) perhaps not even requiring a meeting at all, but decided by a competent individual or by a group using remote communication methods such as email or teleconference. More risky or important decisions might require a face-to-face meeting but use an informal process. At the next level a formal decision-making process might be appropriate, with the most risky and important decisions of all requiring a full facilitated decision-making process supported by specialist decision tools. Having defined these parameters, every decision should be assessed against them to determine the level of decision-making process to be employed.

A3.2 Decide whether to intervene to protect objectives. The assessment step in the Six A's model encourages individuals to decide whether it is necessary to intervene in order to manage a particular group risk attitude. Each individual in the decision-making meeting should seek to be aware of the current risk attitude being adopted by the group and to assess its implications for the decision process and outcome. Such assessments must consider the probability of an adverse outcome arising if no intervention is made, and the size of the potential impact on the decision. As with every aspect of making decisions in risky and important situations, an individual's perception of probability and impact in this regard will be biased by their own personal triple strand of influences including conscious, subconscious and affective factors. The potential for bias can be overcome by having an objective description of the decision purpose and impact.

Assertion

A4.1 Set appropriate meeting culture. The wider organizational culture is addressed by action A1.3, but this must be implemented in the decision-making situation. Here it is important to ensure that individuals in the decision-making group understand and accept the ground rules for the decision process. These include values and behaviours which encourage adoption of appropriate risk attitudes by each participant and by the group as a whole. These behaviours include the cultivation and enforcement of a blame-free environment, which allows open expression of a point of view without inappropriate criticism or recrimination. The meeting setting must allow personal challenge between members of the decision-making group, in a context of mutual respect and trust. The process must focus on the issue not the person, and engage in creative conflict resolution where necessary. It is the role of the meeting leader (or facilitator where present) to set the tone of the meeting at the start, monitor the prevailing culture during the meeting, and ensure that it remains appropriate at all times.

A4.2 Adopt appropriate meeting behaviours. In addition to the meeting culture described in action A4.1, a number of specific behaviours should be practised in decision-making meetings. These are relevant to all meetings, but are particularly helpful in group decision-making situations where the riskiness and importance of the decision might disturb the group's equilibrium. Typical good meeting behaviours include the following:

- clear and defined objectives for the decision, taking account of the effect of framing;

- making the decision context explicit so that participants are aware of all the relevant factors when making their decision;

- allowing free expression of different positions before settling on a group decision, and giving appropriate weight to the lone voice or minority view;

- awareness of sources of bias, exposing these in order to enable them to be countered;

- verbalizing perceptions of risk, allowing participants to express their views freely, equally valuing those perceptions arising from conscious, subconscious or affective sources;

- recognizing the existence of opportunities as well as threats, and treating them equally.

Again the meeting leader or facilitator has a particular role in ensuring that participants are aware of the need to exercise these good meeting behaviours throughout the meeting.

A4.3 Use a facilitator where appropriate. Where a decision is determined to be high-risk and high-importance (using the criteria defined in action A2.1), a competent facilitator should conduct the meeting. This person will understand the sources of influence arising from the triple strand factors, be able to diagnose their presence and effect in a meeting, and have the skills and experience to be able to deal with them effectively. A good facilitator will be recognized as independent of the decision situation, will have (or be able to win) the respect of all meeting participants, and will ensure that the meeting achieves its goals as effectively as possible, without getting in the way of the decision-making process. The facilitator will possess the necessary personal characteristics to model the required meeting behaviours, including a high level of self-awareness, emotional literacy and risk maturity.

A4.4 Challenge inappropriate situations. A number of meeting parameters have the potential to interfere with the decision outcome and can lead to a suboptimal result if they depart from the ideal. It is important that individuals are able to assert their needs and intentions to challenge and correct any factor within the decision-making context if it shows signs of exerting a malign influence. This may include directly challenging any individual participants who might exhibit inappropriate behaviours (such as personal criticism or pursuing a hidden agenda). It also requires challenging the operation of unhelpful group heuristics or cognitive biases (for example, groupthink or cautious shift), as well as identifying any wider aspects of organizational culture that might be adversely influencing the decision process or outcome (such as senior management stated preferences or company policies). The meeting leader or facilitator is usually responsible for making these challenges, which requires a high degree of personal courage, risk-taking and resilience and the ability to be assertive and not aggressive or manipulative. However, any participant in the decision meeting should be able to make the necessary challenge if the leader or facilitator fails to do so.

Action

A5.1 Use power appropriately. Our research has indicated the importance of powerful individuals in the context of decision-making meetings, and their ability to influence the decision process and outcome. As a result it is essential that all sources of power should be explicitly recognized, including not just the formal positional power of the leader, but other individuals whose power derives from technical expertise or a coercive or reward-based position. Powerful individuals should take particular care not to misuse their influence in the decision-making context, and need to exhibit a high degree of emotional literacy (self-awareness, self-management and awareness of others). The meeting leader and facilitator can have a particular role in monitoring and moderating the use of power in the meeting (though they themselves are powerful people!).

A5.2 Prevent propinquity from biasing judgement. Individuals involved in making a group decision need to be aware of the extent to which the decision matters to them personally (their propinquity in relation to the decision), and the effect this has on their behaviour during the decision-making process. Where they detect an inappropriate influence over their risk attitude or conduct in the meeting, they should take steps to modify their degree of perceived propinquity where possible, or alternatively to adjust their outward behaviour in order to counter any adverse influence. As in the use of power (action A5.1), proactive management of propinquity requires a high degree of self-awareness and emotional literacy. This action may also be applied by decision-making groups if they are sufficiently mature and aware to know their level of shared propinquity as a group, though not all groups will be in this position.

A5.3 Retain focus on objectives. It is essential for a decision-making meeting or situation to remain firmly focused on the objectives of the meeting, but this can be very difficult for participants during the cut-and-thrust of an active meeting. Having a statement of the decision purpose, decision-making criteria and other important factors in full view at a meeting can help the group to stay focused. Individuals might use written notes or prompts to help them focus. Objectives are rarely straightforward. Usually there will be competing priorities, and the relative priority of these needs to be understood, typically in conjunction with the analysis of stakeholder needs and expectations. Using interventions to summarize and check can help the group stay on track, reigning in a tendency to get carried away and proceed down a compelling yet ineffective pathway. Retaining focus on objectives sometime requires a willingness to delay gratification. This may mean simply keeping your mouth shut and waiting to see what happens next. It may mean managing your excitement, anger or some other emotion in order to let a situation develop. Conversely it may mean speaking out when the comfortable thing for you to do would be to keep quiet. None of these judgements about personal interventions can be made without a clear understanding of objectives and relative priorities of competing priorities.

Acceptance

A6.1 Define triggers for intervention. Where the assessment step leads to a decision to leave the existing group risk attitude unmanaged, no intervention is made. However individuals in the decision-making meeting should not then relax and become passive. The current situation is accepted, but actively monitored in case intervention becomes appropriate later. This requires an understanding of the trigger conditions under which intervention is required, and individuals should seek to define these in advance of the decision meeting, then apply them continuously during the meeting. Where the existing risk attitude has been accepted without intervention, but one or more of the trigger conditions has been met, the individual should then reassess the need for intervention, by cycling back to the assessment step, specifically to action A3.2, which is to decide whether to intervene to protect objectives.

Alternative views

The previous section lists practical actions to ensure that group risk attitude is managed properly in support of effective decision-making. This list is structured around our Six A's model, identifying how our recommended steps relate to awareness, appreciation, assessment, assertion, action and acceptance respectively. There are however some other ways to think about the challenge of managing group risk attitude in making decisions.

For example, different actions have different time horizons with regard to when they are required to be taken. It is possible to divide the action list into those actions which are long term, those which take place in the short-term, the ones relating to now (that is, the specific time of a particular meeting), and others which are ongoing. This division scheme is shown in Table 7.2.

Alternatively we can relate the recommended actions to a particular decision-making meeting. This allows us to identify which steps need to be taken in advance of the meeting, which are necessary during the meeting itself, and other actions to be performed after the meeting is over. Table 7.3 presents the actions sorted in this way.

Table 7.2   Recommended actions, sorted by time horizon

Time horizon	Relevant recommended actions
Long term and ongoing	A1.1 Develop individuals
	A1.2 Embed organizational learning
	A1.3 Review organizational culture (long term)
	A1.4 Perform stakeholder analysis (common stakeholders)
	A2.1 Define clear criteria for decision-making groups
	A2.2 Promote relative regard
Short term	A1.3 Review organizational culture (current)
	A1.4 Perform stakeholder analysis (specific stakeholders)
	A3.1 Define meeting parameters
	A4.3 Use a facilitator where appropriate
Immediate	A4.1 Set appropriate meeting culture
	A4.2 Adopt appropriate meeting behaviours
	A2.2 Demonstrate relative regard
	A3.2 Decide whether to intervene to protect objectives
	A4.4 Challenge inappropriate situations
	A5.1 Use power appropriately
	A5.2 Prevent propinquity biasing judgement
	A5.3 Retain focus on objectives
	A6.1 Define triggers for intervention

It is important to note that in relation to a particular decision-making meeting, most of the actions relating to the first two A's (awareness and appreciation) should already have been completed. If these have not been undertaken, it is too late to perform them during the meeting itself, and the decision quality is likely to be compromised or reduced.

The purpose of presenting the same action list in three different ways is to emphasize that the recommended practical actions serve a range of purposes. They are inherently right for an organization that wishes to make the best possible decisions, and the Six A's model (Table 7.1) illustrates how the actions map to best practice. These actions also need to be embedded in the daily practices of an organization, as shown by the range of time horizons which they cover (Table 7.2), demonstrating that the challenge of managing risk attitudes in decision group-making is an integral part of all that an organization does. Finally, our recommendations are specifically focused on optimizing the decision-making process, and Table 7.3 shows how they relate to a particular meeting setting.

Table 7.3   Recommended actions in relation to a decision-making meeting

Timing	Relevant recommended actions
Pre-meeting	A1.3 Review organizational culture (current)
	A1.4 Perform stakeholder analysis
	A2.1 Define clear criteria for decision-making groups
	A3.1 Define meeting parameters
During meeting	A4.1 Set appropriate meeting culture
	A4.2 Adopt appropriate meeting behaviours
	A4.3 Use a facilitator where appropriate
	A2.2 Demonstrate relative regard
	A3.2 Decide whether to intervene to protect objectives
	A4.4 Challenge inappropriate situations
	A5.1 Use power appropriately
	A5.2 Prevent propinquity biasing judgement
	A5.3 Retain focus on objectives
	A6.1 Define triggers for intervention
Post-meeting	A1.2 Embed organizational learning

There is also an organizational challenge in deciding how to implement these recommendations. Different readers will want to consider how best the suggested actions should be presented to their particular organization in order to maximize the chances of them being adopted effectively. Some are likely to find one presentational framework more helpful while others might follow another. Indeed we recognize that still further approaches are possible when introducing new methods into an organization, and some creativity is inevitably required if the cultural, behavioural and procedural changes are to be achieved in a lasting and sustainable way.

The most important thing is not how the actions are structured or presented, but how they are implemented. We offer these practical recommendations to the reader, confident that they will help to improve the effectiveness of group decision-making, but we leave each reader to decide how best to move forward in their own unique environment. All we ask is that readers who agree with our diagnosis and prescription should actually take the treatment!

The Journey Continues: Charting the Way Ahead

Sometimes readers are tempted to skip to the end of a book to see how it finishes, find out 'whodunnit', and decide whether it's worth investing time in reading the whole book. Readers who have arrived at this chapter via such a short-cut will have bypassed a rich journey of discovery, and missed both the unfolding of the main path and the intriguing details along the way. Although the key features are evident and can be picked out easily, there is so much more for the thinking reader to find. This final chapter offers a reminder of the significant highlights, identifies some of the things we've discovered during our journey, and suggests some fruitful areas for future investigation.

The journey so far

Chinese philosophers tell us that every journey starts within ourselves. Understanding and managing risk attitude is no different. It is essential for each one of us to know ourselves, to be aware of our own risk attitudes in different situations, and to be able to modify our internal attitudes towards uncertainty where this matters. Only then will we be able to take appropriate risks and make good decisions in risky situations. John Donne reminds us that, 'No man is an island, entire of itself; every man is a piece of the continent, a part of the main' (Donne, 1624). So with risk attitudes, it is not enough to deal with ourselves alone. We each need to understand the risk attitudes of those with whom we work, and manage these where appropriate and possible.

Our work together has provided a structure to enable individuals to do this for themselves and within their working groups, based on the insights of applied emotional literacy. Unlike many consultants' models, we do not propose a simple quick fix. We see a complex web of influences operating on risk attitudes, which we have characterized as the triple strand, representing three distinct groups (as shown in the left side of Figure 8.1). First, there are the overt rational factors which function in the conscious arena, and which can be seen, heard, measured and managed. The second strand comprises a set of subconscious factors, which we might divide into cognitive biases and heuristics, whose influence is hidden. Finally there are a set of affective factors, which are visceral gut-level influences based on instinctive feelings and deep emotions. The three strands are intertwined and connected, and it is hard to distinguish the influence of one over another in a given situation. Nevertheless they represent a rich explanation of the factors which influence risk attitudes in both individuals and groups.

Having addressed the foundational principles of understanding and managing risk attitudes, we have turned our interest to focus on a particular area – group decision-making. This has multiple applications, especially in the business area, where making decisions is a fundamental activity. There is also a natural link to the work on the triple strand, as their influence on risk attitude has a knock-on effect into decision-making (see the right-hand side of Figure 8.1).

It is also a step forward from our earlier work, which helped individuals to understand and manage their own risk attitude as well as that of others. The management of risk attitudes in groups involves more than just being aware of self and others. There are a large number of related influences within a group situation that can affect the decision process and outcome. Many of these are mediated through the risk attitudes of the individuals in the group, and others drive the overall risk attitude adopted by the group as a whole.

Reviewing the existing literature, we found a great deal of work on decision-making theory, a lot written about risk management, and some good academic studies on risk attitude. Our background as practitioners, however,

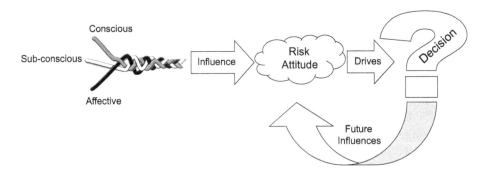

Figure 8.1　The triple strand, risk attitude and decision-making

led us to conduct some focused research seeking to identify the main factors influencing the decision process and outcome when decisions are perceived as risky and important. We formed a hypothesis that propinquity might be a key driver of risk attitude in these situations, and our research explored this suggestion. We found a clearly distinct set of primary factors which influence risky and important decision-making situations, including stakeholders with high power and propinquity, situational factors such as the decision context and organizational culture, and the operation of group dynamics (repeated as Figure 8.2). A range of secondary factors were also identified with lesser influence, though still important.

From the starting point of applied emotional literacy, it is clear that any journey towards managing group risk attitude must begin with *awareness* of oneself and others, supported by a mature and informed *appreciation* of both self and others. These two feed into the formation of relative regard, reflected in the desired transactional analysis state of 'I'm OK; You're OK.' However, this does not necessarily bring us to a place where risk attitudes are properly managed. Sometimes the unmanaged situation will lead to inappropriate risk-taking and a poor-quality decision, in which case we may choose to intervene. The choice over whether such intervention is needed requires us to make an *assessment* of the situation, which might either lead to *assertion* of a required change of course and *action* to achieve that change, or may result in *acceptance* of the existing situation. We have brought these elements together in the Six A's model (repeated in Figure 8.3), which provides a practical approach for understanding and managing risk attitude in group decision-making situations.

Future steps on this journey

We have come a long way from our starting point, and we have discovered much that needs attention. The thinking reader will want to pause for reflection, to consider the new insights and decide how these might be implemented

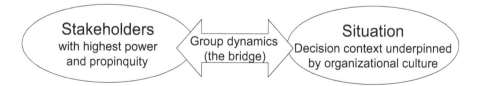

Figure 8.2   **Primary factors influencing group risk attitude**

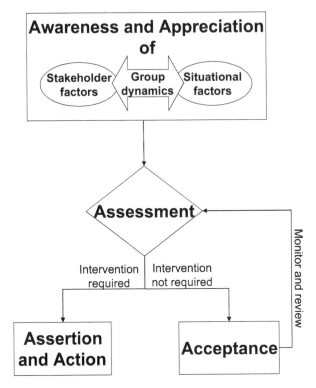

Figure 8.3   The Six A's model

in their specific situation. However, the journey is not over here. As with all investigations, answering some questions has inevitably raised others. Four areas seem to us to be of particular interest and importance:

1.   Our research reported above has provided a dynamic model of the influences on groups which are involved in making decisions perceived to be both risky and important (see Figure 5.8). We have examined a wide range of factors, and proposed a division of these into primary and secondary groups. Within the primary set we have suggested the existence of a lead influence (either a stakeholder with high power and propinquity, or a strong organizational culture reinforced by the decision context). This dynamic model has emerged from our research and experience, and fits the data available to us from these two sources. However, we recognize that there is room for improvement in our understanding of this model, particularly in how the various elements interact with each other. Further work could address this, seeking to clarify and refine the model, and deriving additional practical guidance on how to understand and manage risky and important decision-making in groups.

2. We have learned a lot about the influences on risk attitude
    through the triple strand model. However, we still need to know
    how the triple strand works in practice. Human beings delight
    in pulling things apart to see how they are made and how they
    work, but sometimes we find it hard to put things back together
    in a way that functions properly. DNA researcher Erwin Chargaff
    (1905–2002) warned against this type of reductionism when he
    wrote:

    > *The wonderful, inconceivably intricate tapestry is being taken apart*
    > *strand by strand; each thread is being pulled out, torn up and analyzed;*
    > *and at the end even the memory of the design is lost and can no longer*
    > *be recalled.*

    Chargaff (1975)

    We know that the influences on perception and risk attitude
    include conscious, subconscious and affective factors, but the
    relative importance of these is not clear. We do not know whether
    the interactions between them are fixed or dynamic, situational
    or variable, characteristic of individuals or groups, inherited or
    developed. Given the central importance of the triple strand in our
    work, we believe that it still has secrets and insights to reveal, which
    would justify additional attention and thought.

3. There is considerable looseness of terminology in the field of
    risk psychology, especially among practitioners, and loose talk
    betrays loose thinking. For example the terms 'risk attitude', 'risk
    appetite' and 'risk threshold' are often confused, and wrongly
    used interchangeably. As a result we need agreed definitions
    which distinguish between them unambiguously, indicate their
    interrelationships and dependencies, and clarify their relative roles
    and importance. There are also currently no reliable instruments or
    models to diagnose or measure risk attitude, risk appetite or risk
    thresholds. In all of these aspects, individuals differ from groups,
    so further work is needed to address both, showing how they differ
    as well as identifying common themes.

4. People are aware of the existence of systematic biases, risk
    attitudes and risk appetites within organizations, but it is not
    clear how these come about. A coherent explanation of the origins
    and drivers of organizational risk attitude would go a long way
    towards supporting the effective management of risk at higher
    levels in the organization. It might also lead to new insights into

how organizational development can be encouraged and guided in order to challenge and change any inappropriate risk attitudes or behaviours at organizational level.

While our own fascination with this area remains strong, we invite others to join us on this journey and bring their own enthusiasms and experiences to bear on these important issues.

Setting off on new journeys

In addition to the challenges outlined above which arise directly from the research reported in this book, we have reached a place in our journey that could form a starting point for several new destinations. Figure 8.4 (repeated from Figure 1.4) illustrates the broad range of memberships that each individual maintains as part of human society. Our work to date has addressed risk attitudes for individuals alone, and for those individuals as members of groups in the work context, particularly groups making decisions perceived to be risky and important (highlighted in Figure 8.4).

The figure shows that individuals exist and operate within many other layers, and these should not be forgotten or overlooked. For example the work reported here has focused on the influence of what we have called the primary factors, including stakeholders with high power and propinquity, situational factors such as the organizational culture and decision context, and the operation of group dynamics. We have however also identified a set of secondary factors, namely:

- people with lower power in a decision-making setting;
- societal norms;
- national cultural influences.

These secondary factors are not unimportant; they are just perceived as less significant than the primary set in terms of groups making risky and important decisions. Being 'less significant' however does not mean that these factors will never exert a major influence on decision process or outcome.

Of the secondary factors, there is particular interest in *societal norms*, especially as these have much wider applicability than decision-making groups in organizations. Work is already under way through several initiatives to address risk attitudes in wider society, particularly in the UK. Policy-makers, think-tanks, media groups, professional societies, pressure groups, charities and concerned

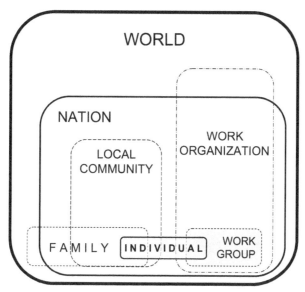

Figure 8.4 Hierarchies of membership and influence (not to scale)

citizens have all started to think about how societal attitudes to risk are formed and reinforced, and how more appropriate risk-taking can be encouraged and promoted across society. Some recent initiatives are mentioned below, not as a complete list, but to indicate the breadth of interest and application.

RSA RISK COMMISSION

One significant current example is the Risk Commission of the UK Royal Society for the encouragement of Arts, Manufactures and Commerce (RSA), launched in 2006. The Commission aims to 'focus on a number of key broad areas such as business, childhood, engineering, healthcare, security and transport … along with cross-cutting thematic investigations'. It intends to work towards 'an integrated framework aimed at guiding people in the principles that they should employ in their efforts to measure and contextualise risk'.

The first area addressed by the RSA Risk Commission in their October 2007 *Risk and Childhood* report (Madge and Barker, 2007) corresponds with one of our own particular interests, namely how children and young people deal with risk in the choices that they make. As children form the society of the future, it is essential that we give them the understanding, skills and support they need to form appropriate risk attitudes and make good choices. Key in this is the role played by parents, teachers and other community leaders across society in releasing or restricting appropriate risk-taking by children. Our own position as parents has caused us to examine how we treat our own children in situations of 'uncertainty that matters', and how we tend to impose our own fears on their innocence. This is of course one area where theory meets reality with genuine personal impact!

The RSA report seeks to 'offer discreet protection but yet encourage healthy risk-taking', and makes six broad recommendations towards this, challenging all stakeholders (government, society, schools and parents) to take action by:

- achieving a balanced view of childhood;

- allowing children more independence as they grow older;

- ensuring more male role models for children;

- encouraging the skills of calculated risk-taking;

- providing cushioned social spaces;

- fully involving the community.

UK BETTER REGULATION COMMISSION

Another significant advance in addressing the role of risk attitude in society was the October 2006 report of the UK Government's Better Regulation Commission entitled *Risk, Responsibility, Regulation: Whose Risk Is It Anyway?* This suggested that:

> *Our national attitude to risk is becoming defensive and disproportionate; the way we try to manage risk is leading to regulatory overkill. There is an over reliance on Government to manage all risks, yet it is neither possible nor desirable to control every risk in life. Personal responsibility and trust must be encouraged. Britain must safeguard its sense of adventure, enterprise and competitive edge. This report recommends a public debate about the management of risk involving individual citizens and the media, but specifically calls for clear and unambiguous leadership from government.*

The BRC report has stimulated wide discussion in a variety of settings, encouraging people to challenge over-regulation, and demanding justification for proposed increases in the regulatory burden. It concluded that society in Britain needs to redefine its approach to risk management, and the report made a number of practical recommendations, including:

- emphasize the importance of resilience, self-reliance, freedom, innovation and a spirit of adventure in today's society;

- leave responsibility for managing risk with those best placed to manage it, and only regulate where this is the optimum solution;

- re-examine areas where the state has assumed too much responsibility for people's lives;

- separate fact from emotion, and balance necessary levels of protection with reasonable levels of risk.

UK HEALTH AND SAFETY COMMISSION

In June 2006 the UK Health and Safety Commission launched an initiative on Sensible Risk Management, saying:

> *We believe that risk management should be about practical steps to protect people from real harm and suffering – not bureaucratic back covering … Our approach is to seek a balance between the unachievable aim of absolute safety and the kind of poor management of risk that damages lives and the economy.*

Their principles are presented in Table 8.1.

These principles have since been implemented widely across national and local government, and are the subject of an audit department who are

Table 8.1   Principles of sensible risk management

(adapted from Health and Safety Commission, 2006)

Sensible risk management *is* about:	Sensible risk management *is not* about:
Ensuring that workers and the public are properly protected	Creating a totally risk free society
Providing overall benefit to society by balancing benefits and risks, with a focus on reducing real risks – both those which arise more often and those with serious consequences	Generating useless paperwork mountains
Enabling innovation and learning not stifling them	Scaring people by exaggerating or publicizing trivial risks
Ensuring that those who create risks manage them responsibly and understand that failure to manage real risks responsibly is likely to lead to robust action	Stopping important recreational and learning activities for individuals where the risks are managed
Enabling individuals to understand that as well as the right to protection, they also have to exercise responsibility	Reducing protection of people from risks that cause real harm and suffering

responsible for ensuring that an unthinking 'health-and-safety culture' does not stifle appropriate risk-taking.

UK GOVERNMENT REPORTS

The role of government in shaping risk attitudes in areas of public policy and practice has been the topic of considerable debate in recent years in the UK. In May 2005 the then British Prime Minister Tony Blair MP addressed the Institute of Public Policy Research in a speech entitled 'Future challenges: Living with risk'. He suggested that Britain was becoming an increasingly risk averse society, and stated:

> We are in danger of having a wholly disproportionate attitude to the risks we should expect to run as a normal part of life. This is putting pressure on policy-making ... to act to eliminate risk in a way that is out of all proportion to the potential damage.

The result has been implementation in policy of the precautionary principle, to legislate for the worst case on the basis that 'It's better to be safe than sorry.' Blair's speech covered a broad canvas, including health and safety legislation, school trips, fear of fraud, 'new science', public health, and the portrayal of risk in the media, and the Prime Minister promised government action on a number of fronts. His intervention was followed by publication of a report in June 2006 by the House of Lords Select Committee on Economic Affairs, *Government policy on the management of risk*, which challenged whether Britain was in fact a risk averse society, and concluded that the precautionary principle was unhelpful and should be more clearly defined or even replaced.

RISK IN SOCIETY: SUMMARY

All of these various initiatives, and others like them, indicate the growing interest in societal attitudes towards risk. While each group has its own areas of focus, and the individual reports discussed above have each made a contribution in the right direction, there remains a need for a more generally accepted understanding of the role of risk attitude in society. A number of important questions must be clarified and addressed, including:

- how to define public risk appetite in relation to various types of risk exposure;

- the factors which influence and shape public risk attitudes;

- the influence of existing societal norms and values on public risk attitudes, and how these change with time;

- how best to manage risk communication in a way that honestly reflects risk exposure while not understating inherent uncertainty;

- the role of the media in both reflecting and shaping public attitudes to risk;

- the role of policy-makers in both serving and protecting the public;

- whether the precautionary principle is a valid basis for decision-making and policy-making;

- the extent to which a compensation culture exists and is justified;

- whether any society can ever be characterized with a single risk attitude, such as saying that 'Britain is a risk averse society.'

There is also a need for understanding to be translated into coherent and direct actions, in such practical areas as:

- education and child safety;

- public health and food safety;

- energy policy, especially nuclear and renewables;

- demographic changes, including housing and pensions provision;

- security and counter-terrorism;

- dealing with vulnerable groups in society.

Our own contribution to this area has been to define the parameters of the discussion, and distil our thinking into ten key concepts, as shown in Table 8.2. These start from our basic understanding of the nature and characteristics of risk, and move through the main insights arising from our work on applied emotional literacy, to a final statement that managed risk attitudes promote effective risk management with appropriate risk-taking. This conclusion, and the concepts in Table 8.2 that lead to it, are equally valid and applicable in the context of the wider considerations of societal risk attitudes discussed above. Looking to the future, we expect to see frameworks such as the Six A's applied to understanding and managing risk in wider society, not just for individuals or decision-making groups.

Table 8.2   Ten key concepts for promoting appropriate risk-taking

1.	*Risk is uncertainty that matters* – different things matter to different people to a different extent in different circumstances
2.	*Risk includes both downside (threats) and upside (opportunities)* – both need to be addressed proactively, to minimize threats and maximize opportunities
3.	*Zero risk is unachievable and undesirable* – all aspects of life involve risk, and require appropriate risk-taking
4.	*Risk has two sides* – uncertainty can be expressed as 'probability', and how much it matters is called 'impact'
5.	*Risk management requires understanding of both probability and impact* – if the uncertain event is very unlikely or it would have negligible effect, it requires less attention
6.	*Risk management is affected by perception* – How uncertain is it? How much does it matter?
7.	*Perception is affected by many factors* – including conscious rational assessment, subconscious sources of bias, and affective inner emotions
8.	*Risk attitude is chosen response to uncertainty that matters, driven by perception* – individuals and groups adopt risk attitudes either subconsciously or consciously, ranging from risk averse to risk seeking
9.	*Risk attitude can be managed consciously* – emotionally literate individuals and groups respond instead of reacting, understanding which risk attitude best meets the specific needs of the situation
10.	*Managed risk attitudes promote effective risk management with appropriate risk-taking*

Managing risk attitude globally

The discussion above has indicated a wide range of areas in society where risk attitudes are important and influential. We have outlined a number of existing initiatives addressing various aspects of this challenge, and shown how our own work fits into this wider setting. However, even this is not the whole story. A closer look at Figure 8.4 shows other levels of context which are relevant. Individuals exist as part of work groups, and also as members of families and local communities. Individuals, organizations, families and communities form part of a national and international picture, and these higher levels exercise subtle influences over their constituent parts. Early research by pioneers such as Geert Hofstede (1992), Trompenaars and Hampden-Turner (1998) and Gilles Spony (2001) have examined national cultural characteristics from a number of perspectives, and useful inferences can be drawn from their work regarding national perspectives on uncertainty and risk. None of these however directly tackles the question of risk attitude, and this remains an open area for future research.

Clearly individuals, groups, organizations and society at large are all likely to be influenced by the prevailing culture of the country in which they operate. As a result one might expect to be able to correlate risk attitudes at these various levels with different national characteristics. There are a number of limitations to this. Foremost of these is the fact that most countries are not monocultures, and multiculturalism has increased dramatically in recent years. These means that there is unlikely to be a single culture within a given country, although a majority perspective may dominate, and it can be argued that the deep underlying national cultural characteristics only change slowly. Second, many organizations are multinational, as are many individuals, operating across a range of countries, and so they are not subject to a single cultural influence. This is why researchers and practitioners alike have chosen to study risk attitudes initially at individual and group levels rather than at the level of society or the nation, although the higher levels undoubtedly have an influence. Future research and thought is required to complete this picture and add the missing piece to understanding and managing risk attitude across all levels.

Final words

The uninitiated might be forgiven for thinking that risk psychology is a simple matter. All one needs to do is define the risk and determine how to respond appropriately. In reality there is much more to consider. A complex web of interdependent factors exerts both hidden and overt influences on individuals and groups, operating at conscious levels, within the subconscious, and via affective feelings and emotions. The research described in this book has shed some light on this complex situation, teasing apart the influences and showing how they relate together. This has allowed us to propose a simple framework, the Six A's, enabling individuals and groups to understand and manage risk attitude, providing a more transparent and robust approach to dealing with risky and important decisions, and laying a foundation for future work. We have enjoyed the journey so far, we have mapped out some visible landmarks for future exploration, and we look forward to continuing the adventure!

Applying the Four A's: Case Study Debrief

Chapter 3 introduced Export Excellence Limited, and told the story of how the senior management team approached a key decision on future strategy, which was perceived by the group members as both risky and important. The story illustrates how the Four A's (Awareness, Appreciation, Assertion and Action) play out in a real-life situation. The debrief presented in this appendix indicates some of the main points which the reader might have spotted in the case study, arranged under the Four A's headings. Following this debrief, a number of more detailed pointers are offered.

Main debrief

Awareness. Paul the PA and Owen from Operations fortunately seemed to be able to see what Theo the CEO and Fiona from Finance were missing, namely the impact of the triple strand of influences on their perception of the risks in the situation and their ensuing risk attitude. Theo's past experience and need to prove that his previous success was not 'just luck' provided a powerful risk seeking cocktail. In contrast, Fiona's belief that Theo was 'just lucky' last time was compounding her tendency for caution into a strongly risk averse attitude. Both Theo and Fiona appear to be influenced more by the emotionally charged memories in their limbic system, than by a rational assessment of the situation and organizational context for the decision. Awareness on their part would have been useful, but this was either absent, or was ignored.

Appreciation. As often happens, the directly opposed risk attitudes of the two senior players resulted in a lack of empathy, inappropriate communication and an 'I'm OK, You're not OK' mindset from both people. Such behaviour destroys any trust that may have previously existed and reduces the ability for flexible, adaptable behaviour to respond to needs. Put-downs, sarcasm and stereotyping can destroy the personal confidence of another, whilst being used to bolster one's own confidence in the situation. Appreciation of opposing views would have enabled a reasonable discussion about differences. Instead, the lack of appreciation compounded the situation.

Assertion. Neither Theo nor Fiona asserted their needs and issues. Instead they chose to be aggressive, with Theo overtly expressing this through objective-setting, use of language and positional power, and Fiona being more passive-aggressive. Conflict handling requires a willingness to resolve and a focus on a 'win/win' approach – both Theo and Fiona were locked into a 'win-over' mindset. Either party could have chosen to break the negative spiral of behaviour, choosing instead to be more optimistic and seek some shared ground. Attention to effective meeting behaviours would have helped this cause. Owen was able to assert his needs and skilfully made a suggestion that enabled Theo and Fiona to save face. Without his mature intervention, the company may have made a poor decision with potentially disastrous consequences.

Action. Although Theo wanted a decision immediately, finding a way forward in the situation required intentionality or delayed gratification to be adopted. In the situation, no one of the senior managers could act alone, each bringing different skills and perspectives to the decision-making table. Displaying interdependent behaviour and general respect for the views of the group as a whole would be key to moving forward. Paul recognized the need for him to remain impartial as he conducted the independent study. There would be personal risks for Paul to take if he was to successfully 'hold the mirror' up to Theo and Fiona and help them to see for themselves the impact of their attitudes to the risky decision. Paul, with Wendy's help, seems to be positioning himself well to address the situation in a very different way. If this is turned into appropriate action and matched with improved emotional literacy from the other key players, the outcome could be quite positive.

Detailed interpretation

It is of course possible to analyze the Export Excellence Limited story in more detail, exposing the influence of specific factors in this risky and important decision-making scenario. Some examples of a more detailed analysis are given below, mapping elements of the story to the items listed in Table 3.1.

The story told in Chapter 3 contains a subplot. In addition to the main decision-making meeting attended by the senior management team which is debriefed in this appendix, the story describes interactions between Paul the PA and his wife Wendy. Although theirs was not a formal decision-making meeting, the couple are in fact confronted with the need to make a decision about their personal future, and both Paul and Wendy show a range of behaviours in response to this risky and important situation. The relationship between this husband and wife is refreshing when compared with the toxic mix demonstrated by the senior management team in the formal decision-making meeting. Paul and Wendy show a positive combination of trust, empathy, relative regard, personal honesty and emotional openness. Paul makes a mature assessment of the challenge he faces in undertaking the independent study, recognizing the need for self-awareness, organizational awareness, empathy, relative regard, assertiveness, optimism and so on. It seems likely that the healthy relationship between Paul and Wendy will provide him with the support he needs to succeed with the study, and will also maximize their chances of achieving their goals as a couple together.

Four generic steps to emotional literacy	Detailed element of emotional literacy	Example in Export Excellence story
1. Awareness	Self-awareness	There is no evidence that Theo or Fiona are aware of what is driving their risk attitude and behaviour in this situation. Much of this meeting seems to demonstrate reaction rather than response, with people acting from the gut and not appearing to be aware of their internal environment. Surprisingly, it is Theo who begins to develop some self-awareness towards the end of the meeting, as his real motives and feelings begin to dawn on him: '*Theo took a deep breath. The truth was that he really wanted to get started in Bulgaria, if only to prove to the others that Brazil hadn't been pure luck. He was getting frustrated with his team's unwillingness to get on with it. He'd always expected opposition from Fiona, who seemed to see the downside in everything. But Owen was right, there was a lot they didn't know about Eastern Europe. And the "neutral study" offered a face-saving way out of confrontation with Fiona.*' Perhaps if the leader of this decision-making group can build on his growing self-awareness and use it as a springboard into developing more emotional literacy, he might achieve his personal and organizational goals more often.
	Organizational awareness	Paul the PA recognizes the different perspectives of the management team, as he is '*trying to work out in his mind who would be the first to speak their mind and challenge the boss*'. By contrast, Theo seems disrespectful and cynical about organizational structure and responsibilities, as he responds to Fiona with sarcasm: '*Is that a valuable contribution from our esteemed Finance Department?*'

Four generic steps to emotional literacy	Detailed element of emotional literacy	Example in Export Excellence story
2. Appreciation	Trust	Trust is clearly lacking between Theo and others in his management team, especially Fiona – at least in relation to this risky and important decision. However, the proposed solution to conduct an independent study relies on being able to trust the person conducting the study, and the whole team recognizes this. '[T]he senior management team considered the options. Who understood the issues, was familiar with the business, and could be trusted by everyone to be impartial?'
	Empathy/relative regard	Theo fails to appreciate others in his team, especially Fiona: 'I always thought it would go well, despite some negativity from the usual quarters.' Owen on the other hand demonstrates a good level of relative regard as he starts his intervention with some positive comments: 'First of all, congratulations on the Brazil success. I wasn't sure it would work at first, given our lack of experience in South America. There's no doubt Megatronic has hit the market and is doing well for us there.' He even attempts to recognize and value the differing viewpoints of the two protagonists, as he says 'It's obvious that there are a number of ways of looking at this situation, and different people will have different views on how best to proceed. You and Fiona are probably both right.'
	Flexibility/ adaptability	Owen seems to be the most flexible of those present at the decision-making meeting, as he makes his intervention into the debate: 'Owen spoke louder than usual, sitting forward in his chair and looking straight at the CEO. Everyone turned their attention towards him. The mild-mannered Operations Director seemed about to do something totally out of character.' It is his willingness to act outside his comfort zone that breaks the deadlock in the meeting and allows the group to move towards a solution.
	Personal power/ self-confidence	Theo appears to demonstrate a high degree of self-confidence, although he may simply be using his positional power to give that impression. 'I knew it would work, so well done to all of you who worked hard to back me on this one.' If he had been truly self-confident he would have allowed a more inclusive approach which welcomed alternative views instead of resisting them. Instead his apparent self-confidence was counter-productive, generating a negative reaction from his colleagues.

Four generic steps to emotional literacy	Detailed element of emotional literacy	Example in Export Excellence story
2. Appreciation	Cultural fluency	It seems that the differences between doing business in Brazil or in Bulgaria were not understood. Theo appears to think that all markets are the same, and is prepared to base his strategic decision on informal opinions and very little hard data: 'Everyone at the golf club is talking about Eastern Europe as the hot place to be, and my cousin's just bought a villa outside Sofia, so I thought Bulgaria would be as good a place as any.' However, when Owen questions this position by reminding the team that 'Bulgaria isn't Brazil, and we ought to be careful before we rush into something that we can't sustain', Theo seems to reconsider: 'The truth was that he really wanted to get started in Bulgaria, if only to prove to the others that Brazil hadn't been pure luck ... But Owen was right, there was a lot they didn't know about Eastern Europe.' Theo is a long way from cultural fluency, but perhaps he is beginning to realize its importance.
3. Assertion	Objective setting	Theo uses his position to set his agenda 'Right everyone, settle down. No time for small-talk, we've got business to do. I hope you're all ready for make some good decisions this afternoon.' But there is no shared agenda for the meeting and this is an inadequate platform from which to manage the conflicting risk attitudes and built a group response. Theo would do well to remember Stephen Covey's (1989) saying that 'private victories precede public victories' and curb his enthusiasm with the intention of bringing his team with him.
	Use of power	This is most evident with Theo the CEO, who uses his position to assert his authority over the group. Right from the outset he takes charge with his opening comments. He reinforces his personal position when thanking the group: 'I knew it would work, so well done to all of you who worked hard to back me on this one.' Theo also seeks to exert his power when responding to the concerns expressed by Owen from Operations, as he says 'No, we've got a strategy that works, we proved that in Brazil. All we need to do is be bold, and do it again. I'm sure it will be fine. I've thought about this a lot, and if we hesitate we'll lose the chance. It feels right somehow, and I don't want to wait.' Fiona from Finance also tries to use both her positional power and expert power to support her view, when she says 'As Finance Director I could never agree to such a risky venture without knowing what's at stake.' This confrontational use of power from two key members of the decision-making group with competing views sets up a potential for conflict in the meeting.

Four generic steps to emotional literacy	Detailed element of emotional literacy	Example in Export Excellence story
3. Assertion	Use of language	There are several places during the meeting where the language appears to be carefully chosen for maximum influence and effect. For example Theo is very positive when describing the South American results, and in making the case to move into Eastern Europe: '[O]ur recent expansion into South America was fantastic. The Megatronic range was a runaway success, beyond most of our wildest dreams ... First-year sales have exceeded our target by 20 per cent, margin is higher than expected due to aggressive local sourcing agreements, and there's a healthy outlook for continued growth into the foreseeable future. Our agent in Brazilia says she's never seen such take up of an imported product ... [S]ince our South American launch was so successful, I think we should build on our momentum, strike while the iron's hot, maintain our first-mover advantage, and take Megatronic into another new market.' This bombardment of facts and rhetoric seems designed to push his colleagues towards what Theo views as the obvious 'right' outcome.

In other places Theo and Fiona use language powerfully to support their entrenched positions, whereas Owen uses language to open up dialogue again. |
| | Goal-directedness | Despite his obvious power-play at the start of the meeting, Theo does successfully set his objectives clearly. '[S]ince our South American launch was so successful, I think we should build on our momentum, strike while the iron's hot, maintain our first-mover advantage, and take Megatronic into another new market.' No-one at the meeting could be in any doubt as to why they were there or what was expected of them. Theo was however unable to put aside his personal risk attitude in the situation in order to lead the group to a shared goal. |
| | Constructive discontent | Fiona is clearly discontented but she seems unable to express this constructively. Her whispered comments are negative and subversive, for example, her first response to Theo's introduction when she says 'Good decisions? You mean doing what we're told, more like.' If Fiona had been able to find a constructive way to share her differing opinion, the meeting would have gone very differently. Owen takes another approach, finding a positive way of expressing his concerns and disagreement, being brave enough to break into a poisonous interaction, trying to make a suggestion that the competing parties could agree upon and offering a constructive solution to move forward. |

Four generic steps to emotional literacy	Detailed element of emotional literacy	Example in Export Excellence story
3. Assertion	Personal openness	Owen is the first to openly acknowledge his feelings about the situation, as he says '*Mind you I'm run off my feet making sure that our ops set-up can meet the unexpected high demand. But I must admit I've got a few concerns about what to do next.*' Fiona initially seems to be hiding her emotions, though she lets them show at times: '*Fiona's voice was harsh as she cut across [Theo].*' Both she and Theo show outward and visible signs of underlying emotion, and Paul notices that '*Theo had turned red and seemed to be getting warm … [he] saw [Fiona's] eyes flash with anger*', but neither Fiona nor Theo are prepared to openly admit or express their feelings. Towards the end of the meeting, Theo does however realize that '*He was getting frustrated with his team's unwillingness to get on with it.*'
	Assertiveness	Much of the meeting is taken up with people being aggressive. Theo and Fiona are the prime examples. Theo states '*I think we should build on our momentum, strike while the iron's hot, maintain our first-mover advantage, and take Megatronic into another new market … What do you think? Any objections?*' Fiona's response is equally aggressive, as she says '*Come on, you can't be serious Theo. I know we've been lucky once, but we can't bet the company's future on another unknown market. What do you know about Bulgaria? Where's the costed launch plan? Who are our in-country agents? What about regulations and local practices? There are too many variables – we've got to do a full risk assessment before we can even think about deciding on this.*' It is this competing aggression between two key players that leads to many of the difficulties in the decision-making situation. Conversely, Owen shows assertiveness in proposing his solution. This starts with his body language: '*Owen spoke louder than usual, sitting forward in his chair and looking straight at the CEO*', and continues with what he says: '*It's obvious that there are a number of ways of looking at this situation, and different people will have different views on how best to proceed … I think we need a period of reflection to consider our options, rather than jumping to a decision today. We ought to focus on the situation and not get personal. It's probably also a good idea to get someone neutral involved who can make an unbiased assessment of the situation and give us some well-defined recommendations. I propose a short focused study…*' By clearly stating the facts and separating the decision-making process from the personalities, Owen prepares the ground for an agreed way forward.

Four generic steps to emotional literacy	Detailed element of emotional literacy	Example in Export Excellence story
3. Assertion	Conflict handling	Owen is the one who tackles the underlying conflict between Theo and Fiona head on. First he addresses the personal issues: '*It's obvious that there are a number of ways of looking at this situation, and different people will have different views on how best to proceed. You and Fiona are probably both right.*' Then he moves to the decision options and exposes the main issues: '*It's a great opportunity for us to explore another market, now that we know from Brazil that Megatronic sells outside UK. Clearly we can't just ignore those facts. But it's also true that Bulgaria is an unknown quantity and there's lots we don't know about doing business there.*' Owen clearly expresses the matters requiring attention and separates the people from the issues.
	Optimism	Theo is very optimistic, as he states '*No, we've got a strategy that works, we proved that in Brazil. All we need to do is be bold, and do it again. I'm sure it will be fine. I've thought about this a lot, and if we hesitate we'll lose the chance. It feels right somehow, and I don't want to wait.*' Unfortunately however his optimism is counter-productive in the situation, since his other behaviours have a mostly negative influence on his colleagues.
4. Action	Meeting behaviours	Owen's assertive suggestions and non-threatening behaviours managed to break the deadlock in what was otherwise a toxic meeting. Unfortunately Theo did not display the basic behaviours needed for effective meetings: keeping on track, encouraging the input of others, using clarification and summary to make sure there was shared understanding, and listening and building on what others said. Owen did show some of these, and managed to rescue the situation, at least temporarily, for example his opening injection into Theo and Fiona's argument: '*It's obvious that there are a number of ways of looking at this situation, and different people will have different views on how best to proceed. You and Fiona are probably both right.*'

Four generic steps to emotional literacy	Detailed element of emotional literacy	Example in Export Excellence story
4. Action	Intentionality	Intentionality in the emotional literacy sense is linked to impulse control and delayed gratification, or the ability to focus with intention on a goal and resist the desire to push to that goal without bringing others along on the journey. Theo's intentions were clear from the outset: *'No time for small-talk, we've got business to do ... since our South American launch was so successful, I think we should build on our momentum, strike while the iron's hot, maintain our first-mover advantage, and take Megatronic into another new market ... we've got a strategy that works, we proved that in Brazil. All we need to do is be bold, and do it again ... I don't want to wait.'* But Theo does not display the intentionality that was required with this team. He made it clear that a quick decision was needed, but his pressing of the issue had a counter effect.
	Resilience	Both Theo and Fiona will need to be resilient in the future if they are to work more effectively together in future decision-making situations. Resilience requires a belief that I'm OK (so you cannot damage me with your put-downs), but also that You're OK (and I just need to understand you better). If decision-makers have relative regard for their colleagues, they are more likely to be resilient when things go wrong for them. In the story, Owen's suggestion of the neutral study provided a 'face-saving way out of the confrontation' from Theo's perspective and an opportunity for Theo and Fiona to stop the destructive pattern of communication if they are both willing and resilient enough to do so.
	Interdependence	Interdependence is the healthy balance between dependence (on others) and independence (which makes others feel excluded). Theo's behaviours are a classic example of where business leaders feel that their position at the top of the hierarchy means they need to be independent (*'lead from the front'*) rather than interdependent (*'leading from within a cohesive team'*). Even when presented with the face-saving solution of the neutral study, Theo continued to immaturely present himself in an independent way, not embracing the opportunity to go forward as a team: *'OK, but who's going to do the study? I'm sure you don't want me to lead it, as I already know the right answer.'* This attitude will make Paul's 'neutral' study very difficult if Theo continues to press his own opinion, failing to see himself as part of an interdependent team. Luckily Paul recognizes this fact.

Four generic steps to emotional literacy	Detailed element of emotional literacy	Example in Export Excellence story
4. Action	Group motivation	Successful decision-making groups are aligned, or attuned to the overriding objectives that the decision needs to satisfy. Closely linked to objective setting, and intentionality, without clear, shared objectives there can be no group motivation, only individual agenda. This final point summarizes the major challenge for Export Excellence Ltd. Nowhere in the story was there evidence of shared objectives and group motivation, only Theo's objectives and everyone else's reaction (Fiona) or response (Owen) to Theo's position. One of Paul's first tasks must be to facilitate the creation of clearly stated, shared objectives for the project. When the group can align around what really matters, it will provide a platform for addressing the risky and important situation and the various perceptions of those risks within the senior management team.

Managing Group Risk Attitude Research Questionnaire

Introduction

Thank you for agreeing to participate in our research into group risk attitude and the influences on group decision-making. We are interested to find out about the factors that influence the perception of risk within any decision, and the processes adopted by the decision-making group in coming to a decision. Your contribution will help to shape our thoughts and inform our writing on this important topic.

We request you to complete the questionnaire below as completely as possible – we expect this may take between 1 and 2 hours. There is no word limit and you can write as much as you wish in answer to each of the questions asked. Honesty and transparency will increase the value of your input, which will remain completely confidential. At no stage of our analysis or writing will you be individually identified.

The questionnaire follows this page. It starts by asking for some respondent information and then continues with five different sections.

The only respondent information we need is the name of your organization, the decision meeting date and the date you responded to the questionnaire. Providing your name and role is optional.

Each question is formatted for either free text with no word limit, or to select responses from a pick-list in a drop-down menu.

Please save your response to any unique file name and return it to us by email.

Thank you again for your time and support.

Ruth Murray-Webster and David Hillson

Respondent information

Name of your organization

Date of decision meeting

Date of response to questionnaire

Your name (optional)

Your role (optional)

Section 1 – Decision objectives and context

1.1   Describe the decision scope and context.

1.2   Outline the explicitly-stated objective(s) for the decision (if any).

1.3   How risky and important you perceived the decision to be.

	Rating *(one of Very/ Quite/ Not very/ Not at all)*	Comment I gave this rating because…
Risky		
Important		

1.4   Were risks (threats and opportunities) considered by you and/or the group before the decision-making meeting?

Self   *(one of Yes/No)*

Group   *(one of Yes/No)*

1.5   Describe any key risks (threats and opportunities) perceived by you and the group before and during the decision-making process.

	Self		Group	
	Threats	Opportunities	Threats	Opportunities
Before decision-making meeting				
During decision-making meeting				

Section 2 – Stakeholders and risk attitude

Complete the table below listing up to 15 stakeholders with an interest in the outcome of the decision. Include all those present in the decision meeting as individuals, including yourself unless you were an observer, and also those of significance but not physically in attendance as either individuals or groups.

Stakeholder (include both individuals present in meeting, and also individuals or groups not present)	Power or Influence on the group and their decision-making process (Not necessarily positional/ hierarchical power) (one of Strong/ Partial/ Weak)	Interest in actively influencing the outcome (one of Active/ Neutral/ Passive)	Degree to which the decision mattered to them personally (one of High/ Medium/ Low)	Preferred decision outcome	Your perception of their risk attitude (see table below for definitions) (one of Averse/ Seeking/ Tolerant/ Neutral)

Term	Definition
Risk averse	Uncomfortable with uncertainty, desire to avoid or reduce threats and exploit opportunities to remove uncertainty. Would be unhappy with an uncertain outcome.
Risk seeking	Comfortable with uncertainty, no desire to avoid or reduce threats or to exploit opportunities to remove uncertainty. Would be happy with an uncertain outcome.
Risk tolerant	Tolerant of uncertainty, no strong desire to respond to threats or opportunities in any way. Could tolerate an uncertain outcome if necessary.
Risk neutral	Uncomfortable with uncertainty in the long term so prepared to take whatever short-term actions are necessary to deliver a certain long-term outcome.

Section 3 – Decision process and influences

3.1   Describe the group decision-making process.

3.2   Considering the decision process and outcome and referring to the stakeholder analysis in Section 2 where relevant, summarize your perception of the influence of the:

   a.   Prevailing organizational culture and expectations.

   b.   People present at the meeting who you rated as having a strong power/influence. Your comments may relate to their risk attitude or the degree to which the decision mattered personally to them, or other thoughts.

   c.   National cultural differences (if any).

   d.   Group dynamics and any notable behaviour expressed by the decision-making group during the meeting.

e.   People present at the meeting who you rated as having a partial or weak power/influence. Your comments may relate to their risk attitude or the degree to which the decision mattered personally to them, or other thoughts.

f.   Wider needs of society, if any.

g.   Any other significant influences on the decision-making process or outcome.

3.3   Present the factors a) to g) in order of your perception of their influence on this particular decision putting the strongest influence first.

Ranking	1st	2nd	3rd	4th	5th	6th	7th
Factor (enter a–g in order)							

Section 4 – Decision outcome

4.1   Describe the decision outcome.

4.2   To what extent do you consider this decision outcome to be optimal?
                    (one of Optimal (good) outcome

                                Reasonable outcome in circumstances

                                Suboptimal outcome

                                Unacceptable outcome)

4.3   Include additional comments to justify your response if necessary.

Section 5 – Post-decision reflection

5.1   Summarize your personal reflections on how the decision outcome was
        reached.

Overt reasons

Hidden reasons

5.2   Rate the strength of influence of the following three factors on the decision process and outcome:

Rational, situational factors, e.g. familiarity, manageability, proximity or personal propinquity ...

(one of Absent/Weak/Partial/Strong/Don't Know)

Subconscious heuristics, e.g. stereotyping, groupthink or risky/cautious shift ...

(one of Absent/Weak/Partial/Strong/Don't Know)

Emotions or feelings, e.g. fear, worry, excitement, revenge, desire to win ...

(one of Absent/Weak/Partial/Strong/Don't Know)

5.3   Any other comments you wish to make on reflection.

Phase 1 Research Decision Data

Phase 1 of the research invited a small number of organizations to share their perspectives and experience of making a specific decision. The questionnaire in Appendix B was used to structure their input. This appendix presents the responses obtained from this phase of the research, summarized and sanitized to protect the confidentiality of our respondents.

A total of eight decisions were analyzed in detail. For five of the decisions, responses were obtained from three different people who had been present at the decision meeting in question. The other three decisions were each described by a single respondent.

The responding organizations included a fast-moving consumer goods (FMCG) company, a team of authors, an internal IT services group, a manufacturing organization in a highly regulated industry, a project management consultancy, a financial services company, and a consortium of higher education institutions (who reported on two different decisions).

Detailed analysis of each decision is presented below, but details of the decisions themselves are not included. The decisions analyzed were commercially confidential and we do not wish to breach the trust of our clients and collaborators in any way. The decisions are presented in no particular order. An overall analysis of the results from the Phase 1 research is given in Chapter 5, and it is intended that this Appendix be referenced when reading Chapter 5 rather than be read as a standalone chapter.

Decision 1

There were ten stakeholders present in the meeting for this decision, of whom three responded to the questionnaire. The decision was seen as being of strategic importance to the organization and very risky in terms of the continued cohesion of the management team; stakes were high.

Of the ten stakeholders, seven were perceived as being powerful by the respondents. Of the powerful stakeholders, two felt strongly about the decision to be made, and these two stakeholders held opposing views about which alternative course of action to choose.

The most influential factors relating to the decision outcome were perceived to be the following:

- The prevailing organizational culture and expectations were seen as most influential. A decision was required that would clearly signify a break from the past and a step change towards a new management style. The decision-making process broke the old organizational cultural norms, but this was explicitly stated as part of the objective for the decision group. It could be argued that this particular aspect of the decision context was the most influential factor.

- The powerful stakeholders were all happy to take a risk in the short term to secure a more certain longer-term future, but they were also concerned about lack of buy-in from some quarters. The stakes were highest for two people but both wanted a clear decision and way forward from the meeting. A decision to defer in any way would have been the least preferable outcome.

- There was a strong leader in the meeting who made it clear that a decision was required, and who worked hard to gain full stakeholder engagement through exploration of different positions.

The decision outcome was judged to be optimal by all the respondents.

There were differences in opinion however regarding the influence of the various elements of the triple strand. Two respondents thought that conscious situational factors had a strong influence, with subconscious and affective factors playing a partial role. One respondent thought that affective factors were strong, with subconscious and conscious factors being only partially influential.

The respondent who perceived strongly influential affective factors was one of the stakeholders who cared most about the decision outcome. They recognized that the behaviour of the stakeholders who cared most was influenced by their feelings. The respondents who perceived the primary influences to be conscious factors were the most senior managers involved in the decision, and neither of them had any personal emotional attachment to the outcome, apart from wanting a clear decision to be made.

Decision 2

Three different members of the decision-making group provided feedback on this decision. They perceived the decision as being very important to the organization and moderately risky. It was an issue where many different people held a variety of opinions about the way forward.

Thirteen different stakeholders were represented in the decision meeting, seven of whom were judged as being powerful by the respondents. All of the powerful stakeholders were perceived as having high propinquity. One of the three respondents was a powerful stakeholder who cared much about the decision outcome. The other two respondents were people who were perceived as having less influence on the group.

The most influential factors relating to the decision outcome were:

- The context for the decision, since there was significant time pressure to make a decision that was significant for the organization, and that would affect a large number of people. In the end the need to decide something drove the process and was more powerful than the entrenched views of some group members.

- The expressed view that the stakeholders with high power and high propinquity dominated discussions, and those with lower (perceived) power did not speak up. This left the impression that 'the sheep would rather follow and accept their fate'.

- The decision was made at a time of great change for the organization and there was a feeling that there were 'bigger things happening', so some people withdrew from the process and let a few people make the decision without opposition.

Two respondents thought the decision outcome was reasonable in the circumstances, and the third thought it was optimal.

All respondents perceived that the most influential part of the triple strand was affective factors (emotions and feelings). Conscious situational factors were a lesser influence, with subconscious heuristics and cognitive bias playing only a partial role.

Decision 3

Only one person from the decision-making group provided a response for this decision, which was seen as being very important and very risky.

Seven stakeholders made up the group in the decision meeting, three of whom were seen as having high power, with one who cared a great deal about the decision outcome.

Three factors were seen to influence the decision outcome:

- The context for the decision, since speed was essential to support the market needs.

- Group dynamics: during the meeting there was robust discussion which challenged both methodology and assumptions. The team became very frustrated and at times almost came to conflict, but by the end they were surprised at the consensus on the outcome. It was felt that a social dinner at the start of the decision-making process had enabled the team to perform well in the actual meeting.

- The outcome of the decision meeting was actually to defer the decision to a later time (some months hence). This allowed the team to agree that the outcome was good, although there were still major underlying differences in opinion.

Affective/emotional factors were seen as being strong, with situational factors having a partial influence and subconscious heuristics or cognitive bias having a weak influence on the process and outcome.

Decision 4

Three members of the decision-making group returned the research questionnaire in this case. The decision was seen as being of moderate importance to the organization and not very risky. (Note: This revealed an implicit assumption in the design of our Phase 1 research questionnaire. We had thought that respondents would automatically choose only to report on decisions that they perceived as risky and important. The fact that the Decision 4 respondents selected a non-risky moderately important decision led us to state explicitly that Phase 2 respondents should only refer to a decision that was seen as both risky and important.)

Nine stakeholders were represented in the decision meeting, with five of them judged as being powerful by the respondents. Of the powerful stakeholders, only one cared especially about the decision to be made. The decision finally made was seen as being optimal.

Factors strongly influencing the decision outcome were as follows:

- The group dynamics were seen as being cooperative and open, so that issues and consequences were discussed openly and challenged positively.

- The organizational culture expected consensual decision-making after extensive consultation – which is what happened.

- A senior manager was awaiting the outcome of the group and would approve the decision. This powerful stakeholder was not part of the meeting but exerted significant influence on the process because the group were acutely aware of the 'customer' for the decision.

When considering the triple strand elements, respondents perceived conscious situational factors as being a strong influence on the decision-making process and outcome. Subconscious and affective factors were perceived as either having a weak influence (by one respondent) or being absent (by two respondents).

Decision 5

The single respondent for this decision saw it as being of great importance to the organization, but did not think that it should have been particularly risky. The decision-making process itself increased the riskiness of the final decision, as personal issues were created resulting in raised stakes.

Five stakeholders were present in the meeting, two of whom were perceived as having high power and caring about the decision outcome. The respondent was not one of these people. The final decision outcome was seen as being optimal by the two high power, high propinquity stakeholders, but the respondent thought the decision was suboptimal.

The most influential factors relating to the decision outcome were:

- The two powerful stakeholders both demonstrated a highly risk averse attitude to the situation. One was the most senior manager in the company, and the culture of the organization determined that this person's opinion would be unassailable. The fact that the other powerful stakeholder agreed with the senior manager's position made the decision outcome cut and dried although there were many other (arguably more favourable and rational) alternatives that could have been chosen.

- The prevailing organizational culture tended to display extreme caution, although sometimes this is inappropriate.

- There were some strong personalities in the group, and the dynamics of the meeting had the effect of polarizing views to some extent.

Both emotions and subconscious heuristics/cognitive bias were seen as having a strong influence on the decision outcome, with rational situational factors having little perceived influence.

Decision 6

One person responded on this decision, which was perceived as being of strategic importance for the organization and very risky.

Fourteen people were present in the meeting. Of these, six were seen as having high power and all of these six also cared deeply about the decision outcome. Two more stakeholders of lower power also cared about the decision outcome to a high degree.

The eight people with high propinquity all wanted the same outcome and were seen as having a risk seeking attitude in this particular circumstance.

The most influential factors relating to the decision outcome were:

- The organizational culture that 'we deliver on our promises'. The decision that was taken achieved that goal, but left significant secondary risks to the business.

- The fact that the most significant stakeholders all agreed and shared a risk seeking attitude. This makes it likely that the decision was affected by the risky shift heuristic.

- The less powerful people at the meeting were more risk averse and had opposing views, but the group dynamics was not conducive to them 'sticking their head above the parapet'.

The decision outcome has proved to be unacceptable. The wider business has been damaged by the decision as a result of risks which were known at the time of making the decision but which were ignored.

When considering the triple strand, the respondent felt that affective and subconscious factors had a strong influence, with rational factors playing a weak role in the process and outcome.

Decision 7

Three people formed the decision-making group for this decision, and all three provided feedback. The decision was perceived as being both important and risky.

The power of these stakeholders was viewed slightly differently by each respondent, but each had a significant influence. All three respondents cared deeply about the decision outcome, albeit for different reasons. There were also a number of high-power stakeholders who were not present in the meeting, but whose interests had an effect on the decision outcome.

The decision outcome was most strongly influenced by the following factors:

- The context for the decision was founded on the previous history of the project, which had experienced multiple deferred decisions, false starts, failure to deliver, changed scope, mismatched expectations, poor communication and loss of trust.

- The group dynamics were important, with one group member initially acting in a facilitating role, but who ended up taking control in a way that left one other participant feeling manipulated.

- The group dynamics were complicated by the fact that the decision-makers were friends who were more concerned to preserve their relationships than with the actual decision being made.

All the respondents reported that emotions were high and that affective factors had a significant influence. Situational factors were also seen as significant. None of the respondents reported any perception of influence by heuristics or cognitive bias.

Decision 8

Three people responded to the questionnaire for this decision, and they all thought the decision was very important, although there were varying perceptions of the degree of riskiness.

Ten stakeholders were present in the meeting, and three of these were perceived as being powerful and with high propinquity. The outcome for these three stakeholders was good, since they got what they wanted. Respondents, however, only judged the decision outcome as being reasonable in the circumstances, not good.

The most influential factors relating to the decision outcome were as follows:

- All the attendees were influenced in their decision by the powerful managers at the meeting. Senior management's desire to change was very clear.

- The decision context that showed that the current arrangements were not satisfactory, even though the way ahead was not clear.

- There was a strong desire to follow a logical decision-making process in order to be able to justify the decision outcome.

All three respondents perceived that rational, situational factors were strong, with subconscious and affective factors playing only a partial role in the decision-making process.

The Web-Based Survey

1. A risky and important decision

Think about an important and risky decision taken, in a meeting setting, by a group you have been part of.

1. **Did you (personally) consider risks overtly before the decision meeting?**

    [▼] (Answer: Yes or No)

2. **Did the group, as a group, consider risks overtly before the decision meeting?**

    [▼] (Answer: Yes or No)

3. **If you answered yes to either of the earlier questions, were the risks that were considered overtly:**

    [▼] (Answer: Threats; Opportunities; Both)

2. The decision outcome

Think about the decision made in the meeting and the extent to which it was an optimal decision given the objectives of the organization.

4. **Was the decision outcome:**

    [▼] (Answer: Optimal; Reasonable; Sub-optimal; Unacceptable)

3. Influences on process and outcome

5. **Please rate you perception of the influences on the decision process and decision outcome against the following factors:**

	strong	partial	weak	none
a) organizational culture	○	○	○	○
b) the people in the meeting with high power	○	○	○	○
c) national culture	○	○	○	○
d) group dynamics	○	○	○	○
e) the people in the meeting with less than high power	○	○	○	○
f) societal norms	○	○	○	○
g) the context for the decision	○	○	○	○
h) the people in the meeting who cared most about the outcome	○	○	○	○

6. Please rank the influences on the decision process and decision outcome. Allocate 1 for the most important, 2 for the next and so on, using all 8 numbers.

	strong	partial	weak	none
a) organizational culture	○	○	○	○
b) the people in the meeting with high power	○	○	○	○
c) national culture	○	○	○	○
d) group dynamics	○	○	○	○
e) the people in the meeting with less than high power	○	○	○	○
f) societal norms	○	○	○	○
g) the context for the decision	○	○	○	○
h) the people in the meeting who cared most about the outcome	○	○	○	○

7. Please rate the strength of influence of the following three factors on the decision process and decision outcome.

	strong	partial	weak	none
Rational, situational factors, e.g. familiarity, manageability, proximity or personal propinquity	○	○	○	○
Subconscious heuristics, e.g. stereotyping, group-think or risky-cautious shift	○	○	○	○
Emotions or feelings, e.g. fear, worry, excitement, revenge, desire to win	○	○	○	○

8. From your experience, to what extent do you believe the influences on this decision to be typical

[▼] (Answer: Typical; Partially typical; Not typical)

Emotional Intelligence/Literacy Diagnostic Tools

APPENDIX

E

Developing emotional literacy is an important aspect of understanding and managing risk attitudes. Many diagnostic tools are available to help individuals understand a range of dimensions of emotional intelligence/literacy, both through self-assessment and via feedback from others. This is a mature market and each of these tools has a sound research base. Similar products to assess risk attitudes are not currently available.

This appendix lists some of the main emotional literacy diagnostic tools, both for the general interest of readers and to assist specifically in the development of self-awareness in individuals (as recommended in Chapter 7). Inclusion or omission in this appendix does not imply endorsement or otherwise of a particular tool. All the tools listed here are questionnaire-based and are designed for self-assessment by an individual as a minimum, and ideally for use on a 360° basis by the individual's manager(s), subordinate(s) and peers.

All information in this appendix was current in November 2007. The relevant company names and web addresses can be consulted for up to date versions.

Diagnostic tool	Researcher(s)	Supplier
Emotional and Social Competency Inventory (ESCI)	Boyatzis and Goleman	www.haygroup.com
Emotional Intelligence Quotient (EQ-i)	BarOn	www.mhs.com
Mayer–Salovey–Caruso Emotional Intelligence Test (MSCEIT)	Mayer, Salovey and Caruso	www.mhs.com
Emotional Intelligence View 360 (EIV360)	Nowack	www.envisialearning.com
Emotional SMARTS	Donaldson	www.emotionalsmarts.com
AppliedEI	Sparrow	www.appliedei.co.uk

References

Association for Project Management (2004) *Project Risk Analysis and Management (PRAM) Guide*, 2nd edn. (High Wycombe, Bucks: APM Publishing. ISBN 1-903494-12-5).

Barsade S. G. and Gibson D. E. (2007) 'Why does affect matter in organisations?', *Academy of Management Perspectives*, February, pp. 36–59.

Berne E. (1961) *Transactional Analysis in Psychotherapy*. (New York: Ballantine Books, reissued 1986. ISBN 0-345-33836-7).

Bernoulli D. (1738) *Exposition of a New Theory on the Measurement of Risk*. (St Petersburg, Russia: Papers of the Imperial Academy of Sciences).

Bernstein P. L. (1996) *Against the Gods – the remarkable story of risk*. (Chichester, UK: J Wiley, ISBN 0-471-12104-5).

Better Regulation Commission (2006) *Risk, responsibility and regulation: Whose risk is it anyway?* (London: Better Regulation Commission).

Blair A. (2005) 'Future challenges: living with risk', speech to IPPR, 26 May 2005. http://www.number-10.gov.uk/output/Page7562.asp accessed 13 November 2007.

Bourne L. (2007) 'Avoiding the successful failure', presented at the PMI Global Congress Asia-Pacific 2007, Hong Kong, January 2007.

Chargaff E. (1975) 'A fever of reason the early way', *Annual Reviews of Biochemistry*, 44, pp. 1–18.

Cherniss C. and Goleman D. (eds) (2001) *The Emotionally Intelligent Workplace*. (San Francisco, CA: Jossey-Bass, ISBN 0-7879-5690-2).

Coleman L. (2006) *Why Managers and Companies Take Risks*. (Heidelberg and New York: Physica-Verlag, ISBN 1-431-194-1).

Covey S. R. (1989) *7 Habits of Highly Effective People*. (New York: Simon and Schuster).

Davis D. M. (1970) *Game Theory: A non-technical introduction*. (Dover Publications Inc.: New York, ISBN 0-486-29672-5).

Donne J. (1624) *Devotions upon emergent occasions: Meditation XVII*.

Druskat V. U. and Wolff S. B. (2001) 'Building the emotional intelligence of groups', *Harvard Business Review*, 79: 3, pp. 80–90.

Dychoff A. (2007) 'Chosen conscious competence ideas', http://www.businessballs.com/consciouscompetencelearningmodel.htm, accessed 30 November 2007.

Finucane M. L., Alhakami A., Slovic P. and Johnson S. M. (2000) 'The affect heuristic in judgements of risks and benefits', *J Behavioural Decision Making*, 13, pp. 1–17.

Fischhoff B. (1985) 'Managing risk perceptions', *Issues in Science and Technology*, 2: 1, pp. 83–96.

Fischhoff B., Lichtenstein S., Slovic P., Derby S. L. and Keeney R. L. (1981) *Acceptable Risk*. (Cambridge, UK: Cambridge University Press).

Gill T. (2007) *No fear. Growing up in a risk-averse society*. (London: Calouste Gulbenkian Foundation, ISBN 978-1-903080-08-5).

Gilovich T., Griffin D. and Kahneman D. (eds) (2002) *Heuristics and Biases: The psychology of intuitive judgement*. (Cambridge, UK: Cambridge University Press, ISBN 0-5217-9679-2).

Goleman D. (1995) *Emotional Intelligence: Why it can matter more than IQ*. (London: Bloomsbury Publishing plc, ISBN 0-7475-2830-6).

Goleman D. (1998a) 'What makes a leader?', *Harvard Business Review*, 76: 6, pp. 93–104.

Goleman D. (1998b) *Working with Emotional Intelligence*. (London: Bloomsbury Publishing plc, ISBN 0-7475-3984-7).

Goleman D. (2001) *Emotionally Intelligent Workplace: How to select for, measure and improve emotional intelligence in individuals, groups and organisations*. (Hackensack, NJ: Jossey-Bass, ISBN 13: 9-7807-8795-690-5).

Goleman D. (2003) *Destructive Emotions*. (London: Bloomsbury Publishing plc, ISBN 0-7475-5393-9).

Goleman D., Boyatzis R. and McKee A. (2004) *Primal Leadership: Learning to lead with emotional intelligence*. (Boston, MA: Harvard Business School Press, ISBN 1-5913-9184-9).

Hammond J. S., Keeny R. L. and Raiffa H (1998) 'The hidden traps in decision making', *Harvard Business Review*, September–October, online version.

Health and Safety Commission (2006) 'Sensible risk management principles', http://hse.gov.uk/risk/principles.htm, accessed 13 November 2007.

Higgs M. and Dulewicz V. (2002) *Making Sense of Emotional Intelligence*, 2nd edn. (Swindon, UK: Nelson, ISBN 0-7087-0367-4).

Hillson D. A. and Murray-Webster R. (2007) *Understanding and Managing Risk Attitude*, 2nd edn. (Aldershot, UK: Gower, ISBN 978-0-566-08798-1).

Hillson D. A. and Simon P. W. (2007) Practical project risk management: The ATOM Methodology. (Vienna, VA: Management Concepts, ISBN 978-1-56726-202-5).

Hillson D. A. (2004) *Effective Opportunity Management for Projects: Exploiting positive risk*. (New York: Marcel Dekker, ISBN 0-8247-4808-5).

Hillson D. A. (ed.) (2007) *The Risk Management Universe: A guided tour*, revised edn. (London: British Standards Institution, ISBN 0-580-43777-9).

HM Government Cabinet Office Strategy Unit (2002) *Risk: Improving government's capability to handle risk and uncertainty*. Report ref 254205/1102/D16. (London: The Stationery Office).

Hofstede G. H. (1982). *Culture's Consequences: International differences in work-related values*, abridged edn. (Newbury Park, CA: Sage Publications Inc., ISBN 0-8039-1306-0).

Hofstede G. H. (2001) *Culture's Consequences: Comparing values, behaviours, institutions, and organisations across nations*, 2nd edn. (Thousand Oaks, CA: Sage Publications Inc., ISBN 0-8039-7324-1).

House of Lords Select Committee on Economic Affairs (2006) *Government Policy on the Management of Risk*. Report ref HL Paper 183-I. (London: Stationery Office).

Howard R. (1988) 'Decision analysis: practice and promise', *Management Science*, 34: 6, pp. 679–695.

Howell W, S. (1982) *The Empathic Communicator*. (Belmont, CA: Wadsworth Publishing Company, ISBN 0-5340-1048-2).

Institute of Risk Management (IRM), National Forum for Risk Management in the Public Sector (ALARM), and Association of Insurance and Risk Managers (AIRMIC) (2002) *A Risk Management Standard'*. (London: IRM/ALARM/AIRMIC).

Jones D. (2007) *'Cotton wool kids'*, HTI Issues Paper 7. (Coventry, UK: HTI).

Kahneman D. and Tversky A. (1979) 'Prospect theory : An analysis of decision under risk', *Econometrica*, 47: 2, pp. 263–297.

Kahneman D., Slovic P. and Tversky A. (eds) (1986) *Judgement Under Uncertainty: Heuristics and biases*. (Cambridge, UK: Cambridge University Press, ISBN 0-5212-8414-7).

Klein G. (2004) *The Power of Intuition*. (New York: Currency Books, ISBN 0-385-50289-3).

Leonard D. and Straus S. (1997) 'Putting your company's whole brain to work', *Harvard Business Review*, July–August, online version.

Lovallo D. and Kahneman D. (2003) 'Delusions of success: How optimism undermines executives' decisions', *Harvard Business Review*, July, online version.

Loewenstein G. F., Weber E. U., Hsee C. K. and Welch E. S. (2001) 'Risk as feelings', *Psychological Bulletin*, 127: 2, pp. 267–286.

Lopes L. L. (1987) 'Between hope and fear : The psychology of risk', *Advances in Experimental Social Psychology*, 20, pp. 255–295.

Lupton D. (ed.) (1999) *Risk and Sociocultural Theory*. (Cambridge: Cambridge University Press, ISBN 0-521-64554-9).

MacLean P. D. (1974) *Triune Conception of the Brain and Behaviour*. (Toronto: Uniiversity of Toronto Press, ISBN 0-802-03299-0).

MacLean P. D. (1989) *The Triune Brain in Evolution: Role in palaeocerebral functions*. (Norwell, MA: Kluwer Academic, ISBN 0-306-4316-88).

Madge N. and Barker J. (2007) *Risk and Childhood*. (London: Royal Society for the Encouragement of Arts, Manufactures and Commerce (RSA) Risk Commission).

Mayer J. D. and Geher G. (1996) 'Emotional intelligence and the identification of emotion', *Intelligence*, 22, pp. 89–113.

Mayer J. D. and Salovey P. (1995) 'Emotional intelligence and the construction and regulation of feelings', *Applied and Preventive Psychology*, 4, pp. 197–208.

Mayer J. D., DiPaolo M. T. and Salovey, P. (1990) 'Perceiving affective content in ambiguous visual stimuli: a component of emotional intelligence'. *J Personality Assessment*, 54, pp. 772–781.

McCray G. E., Purvis R. L. and McCray C. G. (2002) 'Project management under uncertainty: the impact of heuristics and biases', *Project Management Journal*, 33: 1, pp. 49–57.

Murray-Webster R. and Simon P. (2006) *30 Lucid Thoughts from Lucidus Consulting*. (Hook, Hants, UK: Project Manager Today, ISBN 1-9003-91-15-15).

Mythen G. and Walklate S. (2006) *Beyond the Risk Society; Critical reflections on risk and human security*. (New York: Open University Press, ISBN 0-335-21738-9).

Neuberger J. (2005) *The Moral State We're In.* (London: Harper Collins, ISBN 0-00-718167-1).

Nicholson N. and Willman P. (2001) *Fantasy and Roguery: A social psychology of finance risk disasters. Mastering Risk Volume 1: Concepts,* edited by James Pickford, pp. 241–245. (Harlow: Pearson Education, ISBN 0-2736-5379-2).

Project Management Institute (2004) *A Guide to the Project Management Body of Knowledge (PMBoK®),* 3rd edn. (Philadelphia, PA: Project Management Institute, ISBN 1-930699-45-X).

Salovey P. and Mayer J. D. (1990) 'Emotional intelligence', *Imagination, Cognition, and Personality,* 9, pp. 185–211.

Salovey P. and Sluyter D. J. (1997) *Emotional Development and Emotional Intelligence.* (New York: Basic Books).

Salovey P., Brackett M. A. and Mayer J. D. (2004) *Emotional Intelligence: Key readings on the Mayer and Salovey model'.* (Port Chester, NY: National Professional Resources Inc., ISBN 1-8879-4372-2).

Schein E. H. (2004) *Organisational Culture and Leadership,* 3rd edn. (Chichester, UK: Jossey-Bass, ISBN 0-7879-6845-5).

Slovic P. (2000) *Perception of Risk.* (London: Earthscan Press, ISBN 1-85383-528-5).

Slovic P., Finucane M. L., Peters E. and MacGregor D. G. (2004) 'Risk as analysis and risk as feelings: some thoughts about affect, reason, risk and rationality', *Risk Analysis,* 24: 2, pp. 311–322.

Spony G. (2001) 'The development of a work-value model assessing the cumulative impact of individual and cultural differences on managers' work-value systems', *International Journal of Human Resource Management,* 14: 4, pp. 658–679.

Steiner C. and Perry P. (1997) *Achieving Emotional Literacy: A personal program to increase your emotional intelligence.* (London: Hearst Books, ISBN 0-380-9759-12).

Steiner C. (2003) *Emotional Literacy: Intelligence with a heart.* (Fawnskin, CA: Personhood Press, ISBN 1-932-1810-24).

Trompenaars F. and Hampden-Turner C. (1998) *Riding the Waves of Culture*, 2nd edn. (New York: McGraw-Hill, ISBN 0-7863-1125-8).

Trompenaars F. (2004) *Managing Change Across Corporate Cultures*. (Oxford: Capstone Publishing Limited, ISBN 1-84112-578-4).

Tversky A. and Kahneman D. (1971) 'Belief in the law of small numbers', *Psychological Bulletin*, 76, pp. 105–110.

Tversky A. and Kahneman D. (1973) 'Availability: a heuristic for judging frequency and probability', *Cognitive Psychology*, 5, pp. 207–232.

Tversky A. and Kahneman D. (1974). 'Judgement under uncertainty: heuristics and biases', *Science*, 185, pp. 1124–1131.

Tversky A. and Kahneman D. (1981) 'The framing of decisions and the psychology of choice', *Science*, 211, pp. 453–458.

Tversky A. and Kahneman D. (1992) 'Advances in prospect theory: cumulative representation of uncertainty', *J Risk and Uncertainty*, 5, pp. 297–323.

Virine L. and Trumper M. (2008) *Project Decisions. The art and the science*. (Vienna, VA: Management Concepts, ISBN 978-1-56726-217-0).

Weisinger H. (2000) *Emotional Intelligence at Work*, 2nd edn. (San Francisco, CA: Jossey-Bass, ISBN 0-7879-5198-6).

Xie X-F (2003) 'Risk perception and risky choice: situational, informational and dispositional factors', *Asian Journal of Social Psychology*, 6, pp. 117–132.

Index

Risk Doctor & Partners
Company Services

www.risk-doctor.com

tel. +44(0)7717 665222

Risk Doctor & Partners provides *specialist risk management consultancy and training* from Dr David Hillson and senior associates who offer a high-quality professional service to clients across the globe. David Hillson is recognized internationally as a leading thinker and expert practitioner in risk management, and he is a popular conference speaker and regular author on the topic. Risk Doctor & Partners embodies David's unique ethos, blending leading-edge thinking with practical application and providing access to the latest developments in risk management best practice. Full details of the business are at www.risk-doctor.com.

Risk Doctor & Partners also maintains a network of people interested in risk management who want to keep in touch with latest thinking and practice. Risk Doctor Network members receive regular email briefings on current issues in risk management. Previous briefings can be downloaded from the website and are available in English, French, German, Spanish and Chinese. Many of David's papers can also be downloaded from the website.

The services offered by Risk Doctor & Partners include:

- **Coaching and mentoring**, providing personal input and support to key individuals or small teams, aiming to share and transfer expertise.

- **Organizational benchmarking**, using proven maturity model frameworks to understand current risk management capability in terms of risk culture, processes, experience and application, then defining realistic and achievable improvement targets, and action plans to enhance capability.

- **Process review**, comparing your risk management approach against best practice and recommending practical improvements to meet the specific challenges faced by your business.

- **Risk review**, assessing the risk exposure of your bid, project, programme or strategy, identifying and prioritizing threats and opportunities, and developing effective responses to optimize project performance and achievement of objectives.

- **Risk training**, offering a range of learning experiences designed to raise awareness, create understanding and develop skills, targeting senior management, programme/project managers, project teams and risk practitioners.

Lucidus Consulting
Company Services

www.lucidusconsulting.com

tel. +44(0)207 060 2196

Lucidus Consulting provides services from Ruth Murray-Webster, Peter Simon and selected associates to assist in the proper application of project and programme management. True to the name Lucidus, the company aims to create value by *shedding light on managed change*. To achieve this aim, the Lucidus Consulting team does three things.

- First, we provide practical advice and assistance based on intuitive and concise analysis of current situations.

- Second, we enable individuals and teams to take charge of their own change agenda by providing targeted assessment and development of competency.

- Third, we are able to practice what we preach, by providing timely and valuable interim management support to clients.

In addition, we publish monthly *Lucid Thoughts* on our website and in the UK project management journal *Project Manager Today*. *Lucid Thoughts* are personal reflections on an aspect of project or programme management upon which we have a particular and sometimes controversial view. Feedback from *Lucid Thoughts* readers encourages networking and debate on some of the hot topics related to managed change in organizations.

As one of the managing partners within Lucidus Consulting, Ruth Murray-Webster brings her particular fascination with the impact of human beings on organizational change to the company. If people make projects work then understanding human behaviour when working to deliver unique objectives through a transient, multi-functional team of people within the constraints of time, cost and specification must be a priority. Risk attitudes, as explored in this book, form an important part of this story.

Full details of the business are at www.lucidusconsulting.com. The website also offers Ruth's papers for download as well as a full set of *Lucid Thoughts*.

Managing Group Risk Attitude in Action

David Hillson and Ruth Murray-Webster personally deliver a suite of interventions designed to help people to put into action the ideas covered in 'Managing Group Risk Attitude', and in their previous book published by Gower 'Understanding and Managing Risk Attitude'.

The starting place for everyone interested in developing their ability to manage risk attitude is the *1-Day Understanding Risk Attitude Workshop*.

Facilitated by both David and Ruth, the seminar covers all the main themes and learning contained within the book in a practical and fun way. Designed for a maximum of 12 people, the workshop requires no previous knowledge or experience of risk attitudes or emotional literacy. However, people who have already read the books will gain further insights into the ideas presented and gain maximum value from the workshop.

If you are interested in booking on to a public programme, or arranging an in-house programme for your organisation then contact us by email on training@risk-attitude.com

For those who have completed the Understanding Risk Attitude Workshop there are two options for support with *Managing Risk Attitude.*

For individuals, David and Ruth offer a *1-1 Coaching Day* where they support the person as they work through a process of understanding and managing their own risk attitude in respect of a particular uncertain situation.

For decision-making groups, David and Ruth offer *Team Coaching Workshops* where the members of a group facing a risky and important decision can together work through the process of understanding and managing their group risk attitude.